BENALM.
TRAVEL GUIDE

The Updated Guidebook to the Heart of Andalusia's Paradise, Hidden Gems, and Delightful Sun-Kissed Adventures.

Willie Robbins

Copyright © 2024 by Willie Robbins

All rights reserved. No part of this book may be reproduced in any form or by any electronic or mechanical means, including information storage and retrieval systems, without permission in writing from the publisher, except by a reviewer who may quote brief passages in a review.

The information in this book is true and complete to the best of our knowledge. All recommendations are made without guarantee on the part of the author or publisher. The author and publisher disclaim any liability in connection with the use of this information.

Table of Contents

INTRODUCTION 8
Brief History 9
What Makes Benalmádena Special 9
Why Visit Benalmádena? 10
How to Use This Guide 11

CHAPTER 1 12
Planning Your Benalmádena Adventure 12
Best Time to Visit Benalmádena 12
Seasons and Weather Tips 13
Navigating Visa requirements 14
Who Needs a Visa? 14
Types of Visas 14
Application Process 15
Tips For a Smooth Process 15
How to Get to Benalmádena 16
Travel Kits and Packing Essentials 16
Essentials for All Travelers: 17
Safety Instruments 18

General Road Rules in Spain 20
Accommodation Options 21

CHAPTER 2 24

Navigating Benalmádena 24
Getting Around Benalmadena 24
Car Rentals 25
Tips for Car Rental 25
Best Places to Rent Cars 25
Transportation Tips 27
Communication and Connectivity 28
Communication Tips 29
Basic Communication Words and Pronunciation 30
Currency, Cards, Tipping and Tax Information 34
How to Save Money in Benalmádena 36
Useful Apps and Resources 37

CHAPTER 3 39

Where to Stay 40
Luxury Stays 41
Budget-Friendly Stays 44
Unique Stays 47
Romantic Stays 50

CHAPTER 4 54

Discover Benalmádena Wonders 54
Things To Do 54
Top Attractions: 55
Puerto Marina Benalmadena 55
Benalmadena Pueblo (the Old Village) 55
Plaza Espana 56
Parque De La Paloma 57
Teleferico de Benalmadena 57
Butterfly Park, Benalmadena 58
Castillo de Colomares 59
Selwo Marina 60
Bil-Bil Castle (Castillo de El-Bil-Bil) 60
Stupa of Enlightenment in Benalmádena 61
Sea Life Benalmádena 62
Garden of Eagles 63
Malapesquera Beach 63
Golf Torrequebrada 64
Culture House Benalmádena (Casa de la Cultura) 65
Playa Arroyo de La Miel 65
6 Hidden Gems for the Adventurous Souls: 66

Cultural Experiences and Shows 70
   Flamenco Benalmádena 70
   Semana Santa (Holy Week) 70
   Corpus Christi 71
   San Juan Fair 71
   Benalmádena Summer Festival 72
   Veladilla del Carmen 72
   Festival of the Virgen de la Cruz 72
Nightlife and Entertainment 73
   Bars, Clubs, and Live Entertainment: 73
   Tourist Traps to Avoid 78

CHAPTER 5 .... **102**
   Day Trips from Benalmádena 102
      Málaga 102
      Fuengirola 103
      Mijas Pueblo 104
      Marbella 104
      Nerja 105
      Caminito del Rey 106
      Ronda 107
      Gibraltar 108

Granada 109
Tarifa 109
Torremolinos 110

CHAPTER 6 .... **82**

Experiencing Benalmádena's Delights 82
What to eat 82
Popular Andalusian Dishes You Should Try: 82
Local Dining Options 83
Fine Dining Options 90
Budget Dining 92
Cuisine Adventures 95
Spanish Cooking Lessons: 96
Argentinian Flavors 96
Taste of Northern Spain 97
Wine & Dine 97
Shopping in Benalmádena 98
Bargaining Tips and Shopping Etiquette 100

CHAPTER 7 .... **102**

Ensuring a Safe and Enjoyable Stay 112
Staying Safe and Legal 112

Cultural Etiquettes & Customs 113
Religious practice and etiquette 113
Health Tips and Insurance 113
Hygiene: Staying Fresh and Clean 116
Emergency Contacts 118
Sustainability Tips for Responsible Travel in
Benalmádena 119

Benalmadena Map

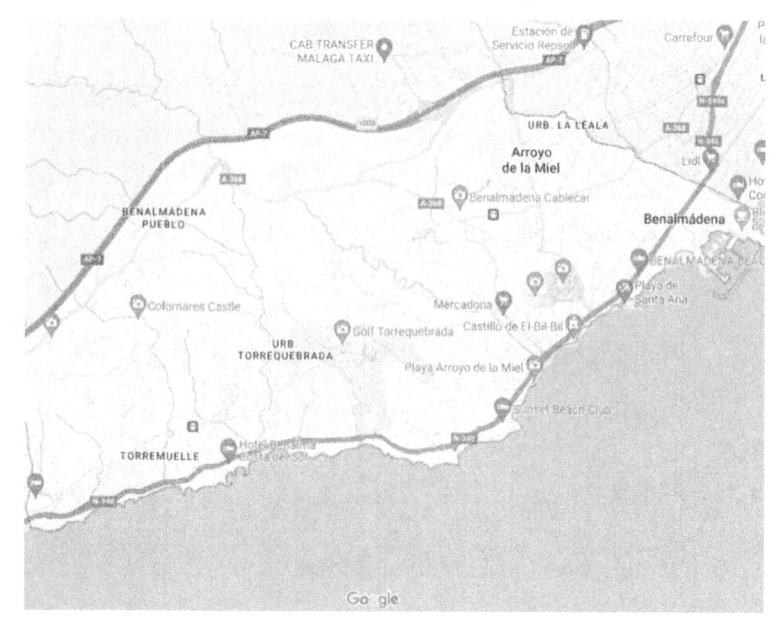

https://maps.app.goo.gl/LDLLZ7brMcY3QwwQ7

INTRODUCTION

Bienvenido a Benalmádena (Welcome to Benalmádena), the jewel of Spain's Costa del Sol, a bustling town where the sun embraces the Mediterranean Sea and history whispers through the streets. Located between the bustling city of Málaga and the energetic town of Torremolinos, Benalmádena is a treasure trove of experiences waiting to be discovered.

Location

Benalmádena is located in the province of Málaga, in the autonomous community of Andalusia. Situated on Spain's southern coast, Benalmádena enjoys a beautiful location surrounded by more than 27 square kilometers of diversified terrain. Its strategic location between the turquoise waves of the Mediterranean Sea and the rocky peaks of the Sierra de Mijas offers a stunning backdrop. The area boasts a unique location that has drawn tourists for ages. It offers expansive vistas that reach to the horizon, where the sea and sky swirl with color. The town's landscape is as diverse as it is breathtaking, from the tranquil peaks of the Sierra de Mijas that attract explorers to the turquoise waves of the Mediterranean that lure sun-seekers.

Weather Conditions

Benalmádena enjoys a subtropical Mediterranean climate that provides over 300 days of sunlight every year. Summers are pleasant and inviting, ideal for lazy afternoons by the pool or refreshing dips in the sea. Winters are moderate, enabling you to enjoy outside eating without freezing. The sunny summers and mild winters provide visitors with excellent weather regardless of the season. This ideal weather fosters a way of life where being outside is not only possible but a daily experience.

Brief History

Benalmádena has a rich and lively history spanning centuries. It was once a small fishing town but has now become a popular tourist attraction. Benalmádena has been changed over time by numerous civilizations, notably the Phoenicians, Romans, and Moors, all of whom left their stamp on the city's culture and architecture. However, Benalmádena prospered most during the Moorish era, notably between the 8th and 15th centuries. During the Moorish era, the town saw great prosperity as a thriving fishing village and commercial station, drawing traders from all over the Mediterranean region with its advantageous position. Today, tourists can explore the charming old town with its small cobblestone streets and whitewashed buildings, see the magnificent Castillo de Colomares, or take in the breathtaking views from the famous Benalmádena cable car.

What Makes Benalmádena Special

What makes Benalmádena unique is its ability to provide a slice of Spain untouched by time along with modern luxuries. One minute you can enjoy the cosmopolitan flare of Puerto Marina, and the next you can stroll through the cobblestone streets of Benalmádena Pueblo, the old village with its whitewashed buildings and flower-laden balconies, and then the same evening eat dinner at a five-star restaurant by the sea. The town is home to Europe's biggest Buddhist stupa, symbolizing peace and diversity, as well as attractions like Tivoli World and Sea Life Aquarium, which guarantee enjoyment for people of all ages. Let's not forget about the hidden gems, such as the Butterfly Park, where hundreds of butterflies form a colorful kaleidoscope.

Why Visit Benalmádena?

Tourists are drawn to Benalmádena's captivating blend of cultural diversity, leisure activities, and natural beauty. There's something for everyone, be it the beauty of the marina, the splendor of the sandy beaches, or the pull of the lush gardens of Parque De La Paloma. Every mouthful from the town's culinary scene delivers a flavor of Andalusia, and the lively nightlife makes sure the good times don't end when the sun sets.

The Culture

Benalmádena is a cultural melting pot where fiestas and siestas are part of everyday life. It is in the swirl of the flamenco dancer, in the tapas that entice your palate, and in the festivals that light up the streets with laughter and music. The people of Benalmádena exude joie de vivre and make each guest feel at home with their gracious welcome. The town hosts events such as the Feria de Benalmádena, which combines flamenco, gastronomy, and celebration to create a breathtaking exhibition of regional traditions, to honor its heritage. Benalmádena's culture is a celebration of food, colors, and festivities. It is a culture that invites you to participate, dance, eat, and live.

Laws and Instructions

Benalmádena is a welcome and safe destination for visitors. Respect for the environment and culture is the main emphasis of these straightforward regulations. It's a location that values its legacy and encourages visitors to do the same.

How to Use This Guide

Getting around: The table of contents allows you to quickly find the information you need. This guide covers everything you need, from lodging to restaurants and hidden gems.

Practical Tips: Get crucial tips on transportation, language, currency, safety, and more to ensure your trip goes smoothly.

Useful Resources: This guide includes maps, applications, websites, and contact information to help you enjoy your time in Benalmádena even more.

In this travel guide, I will share with you the best attractions, hidden gems, activities, and tips to make the most of your visit. You will learn how to get around, where to stay, what to eat, what to see and do in Benalmádena, and more.

Benalmádena awaits your arrival—the scent of orange blossoms, the taste of salt on your lips, and the echo of laughter in its cobblestone streets. Whether you desire sun-soaked leisure or cultural immersion, this coastal beauty will leave you with memories that will last as long as the Andalusian sunsets do.

CHAPTER 1

Planning Your Benalmádena Adventure

An adventure to Benalmádena takes you into a world where the sun shines brighter, the sea sparkles clearer, and the air is filled with the promise of lasting memories. Planning is essential for making your trip as magical as the destination.

Best Time to Visit Benalmádena

Benalmádena's charm shines all year, but for the best combination of pleasant weather and exciting activities, visit between April to June or September to November. These times provide an ideal balance of pleasant temperatures, minimal precipitation, and fewer crowds, allowing you to explore the town's attractions at your own pace. For sunseekers, the peak summer months of June to August are the hottest, with August being the warmest, with average daily maximums of 32°C. However, remember that this is also peak tourist season in Benalmádena.

Seasons and Weather Tips

Spring (March–May): The air is filled with the scent of blooming flowers, and the town begins to come alive. It's time to take relaxing strolls through the streets and enjoy the outdoor cafes.

Summer (June–August): Benalmádena basks in the glory of the Mediterranean sun. Golden sands and water sports entice people to the beaches. It's peak season, so expect a buzzing atmosphere.

Autumn (September–November): The town turns a golden hue as the temperature drops. The sea remains warm enough to swim, and the cultural calendar is filled with festivals.

Winter (December to February): The cooler months bring a more relaxed pace. It's a time for cultural exploration and sampling local cuisine without having to wait in line.

Weather Tips

Sun Protection: Regardless of the season, the Andalusian sun demands respect. Always wear sunblock, a hat, and sunglasses.

Hydration: Carry a bottle of water with you when you explore, especially during the warmer months.

Layering: Evenings can be cool, especially during the shoulder seasons. Layer up to keep warm as the weather changes.

Rainy Days: Although uncommon, rain can surprise you. A small umbrella or a light raincoat can be a trip-saver.

Navigating Visa requirements

Navigating the visa requirements for your trip to Benalmádena is an important step in planning your adventure. Given that Benalmádena is in Spain, the normal Schengen Area procedures apply for obtaining a visa.

Who Needs a Visa?

Non-EU citizens may need a Schengen Visa to enter Spain. This includes tourists from countries that do not have a visa waiver agreement with the Schengen states. Check the current list of countries requiring a visa at the nearest Spanish embassy or consulate or the website of the Ministry of Foreign Affairs, European Union and Cooperation at https://rb.gy/al26yz

Types of Visas

Tourist Visa: For those planning a short-term stay of up to 90 days (about 3 months) within 180 days (about 6 months).

Long-Stay Visa: If you plan to stay for an extended period, you must apply for a visa specific to your purpose of stay.

Application Process

1. Application Form: Fill out the Schengen Visa application form, which can be downloaded from the official embassy website at https://blsspainvisa.com/

2. Documentation: Gather all required documents, such as a valid passport, travel itinerary, proof of accommodation, travel insurance, and financial means.

3. Appointment: Make an appointment with the Spanish Embassy or Consulate in your home country.

Interview: Go to the interview for your visa, where you will present your paperwork and give a biometric sample.

Tips For a Smooth Process

Apply Early: For a short-stay visa, apply at least 15 days (about 2 weeks) before your trip, but no more than six months in advance.

Insurance: Make sure your travel insurance covers at least €30,000 in medical expenses and repatriation.

Proof of Return: Provide evidence of your intention to return, such as a return flight ticket.

Visa regulations can change, so it is important to check the most recent information before applying.

How to Get to Benalmádena

Benalmádena is easily accessible, whether you are flying in from afar or traveling locally. This is how you get there:

Internationally:

Benalmádena is served by Málaga-Costa del Sol Airport (AGP), which is one of the busiest in Spain. To get to your sunny destination, take a taxi or rent a car from the airport, which is only 20 minutes away. If you prefer public transportation, trains and buses run frequently between the airport and Benalmádena, ensuring a seamless transition from air to land.

Locally:

If you are already in Spain, Benalmádena is easily accessible by road and rail. The AP-7 highway is a fast route with tolls, whereas the A-7 Mediterranean highway is toll-free. Both highways connect major cities with Benalmádena, making it accessible to road travelers. The town also has a regular train service from Málaga and other nearby cities to the train station in Arroyo de la Miel. In addition, the local bus system provides a low-cost way to get around town.

Travel Kits and Packing Essentials

When leaving for Benalmádena, packing wisely is just as important as planning your itinerary. Your travel kit should be a customized collection of essentials that are appropriate for the region's climate, planned activities, and personal needs. Here's a guide to help you pack effectively for your adventure.

Essentials for All Travelers:

Travel documents: passport, visa, insurance, and itinerary.

Money: Credit/debit cards and some local currency.

Clothing: Light, breathable fabrics for the day, plus a warm layer for cooler evenings.

Footwear: Comfortable walking shoes and beach sandals.

Sun Protection: wide-brimmed hats, sunglasses, and sunscreen with a high SPF.

Hydration: A reusable water bottle to help you stay hydrated while on the go.

Seasonal Items:

Spring/Summer: Swimsuit, beach towel, and light clothing.

Autumn/Winter: An umbrella and a waterproof jacket in case of unforeseen downpours.

Health and Safety:

First Aid Kit: Essential supplies for minor injuries or illnesses.

Medications: Prescription drugs and any over-the-counter remedies you frequently use.

Hand Sanitizer: To protect yourself from germs while you explore.

Tech Gear:

Phone/Camera: Capture memories without missing a beat.

Chargers and adapters: Make sure they are compatible with Spanish outlets. Types C and F are widely used in Spain.

Portable Power Bank: Charge your devices while on the go.

Extras for comfort:

Travel Pillow: To ensure a relaxing trip to and from your destination.

Earplugs and an eye mask: These will help you sleep soundly in new environments.

Snacks: Nonperishable items that provide a rapid energy boost when needed.

Packing is a matter of preference, and what is essential for one traveler may be unnecessary for another. Create your ideal travel kit by taking into account your comfort, the length of your stay, and the things you intend to do.

Safety Instruments

You must stay safe while enjoying Benalmádena's attractions. Here's a brief overview of the safety devices and precautions you should take:

Personal Safety Instruments:

Travel insurance: A must-have for any unexpected events.

Emergency Contact Numbers: Make a list of local emergency contacts, including the nearest embassy or consulate.

Copy of important documents: Bring a photocopy of your passport and visa.

Safety Tips:

Awareness: To avoid pickpocketing, keep an eye out in crowded areas.

Drugs: Exercise caution and avoid marginal areas.

Night Safety: Benalmádena is safe at night, but it's best to stick to well-lit, populated areas.

Beach Safety:

Blue Flag Beaches: Look for beaches that have been designated as Blue Flag for cleanliness and safety.

Swimming: Follow the flag warnings for swimming conditions.

Road Safety:

Driving: If you are driving, familiarize yourself with the local traffic laws.

Public Transportation: Take reputable taxis or official public transportation.

General Road Rules in Spain

- In Spain, cars drive on the right side of the road.
- Safety belts are required for all passengers in the front and rear seats of an automobile.
- Speed limits apply to all roads. On dual carriageways and highways, the speed limit is 120 km (about 74.56 mi)/h; on all other roads, it is 90 km (about 55.92 mi)/h; and in residential zones, it is 30 km (about 18.64 mi)/h. Speed cameras are widely used in Spain, and the last thing you want is to get fined.
- Driving in Spain requires a minimum age of 18, and renting a car requires a minimum age of 21.
- Talking on a phone or using one while driving is illegal. The use of screen-based navigation devices is likewise restricted.
- Overtaking is only possible from the left side of the car you wish to pass.
- Don't drive after drinking. Blood alcohol levels cannot exceed 0.5 g/l (0.25 mg/l in exhaled breath). Spain has strong drunk driving laws and punishments, and a high blood alcohol level may put you in jail.

- Parking on public roadways is not always legal or free. Many cities have parking restrictions and charge for them. These are often characterized by parking meters.
- Do not park near a yellow line in residential areas. In that instance, you will most likely be towed, especially if you are driving a foreign vehicle.
- Children must always use an authorized restraint system and cannot sit in the front seat if their height is less than 135 cm (about 4.43 ft). It is recommended that kids utilize a backless restraint until they reach 150 cm (about 4.92 ft) or taller. If you wish to transport a baby in a taxi, you must carry an authorized restraining device with you since the same standards apply to taxis.

Accommodation Options

Benalmádena has a wide variety of lodging options to suit every traveler's needs. Benalmádena offers a wide range of accommodations, from beachside properties to modest apartments, ensuring that every visitor finds their ideal home away from home. This coastal town has accommodations for everyone, whether you want to stay in luxury or on a budget. Remember to book ahead of time, especially during peak seasons, to secure your preferred accommodation.

Luxury stays: For those seeking luxury, the Vincci Selección Aleysa Boutique & Spa provides a lavish experience complete with stunning sea views and top-notch amenities. Another luxurious option is the Estival Torrequebrada, which is known for its elegant rooms and exceptional service.

Mid-Range Comfort: You can stay in comfortable and stylish accommodations such as the Benalmadena Jupiter - SunSea Apartments, which offer modern amenities and are conveniently located near attractions.

Budget-Friendly: For the budget-conscious, there are numerous well-rated options, such as the Comfy Studios Benalmádena, which provide cozy accommodations with basic amenities, ensuring a pleasant stay without breaking the bank.

Unique Stays: Consider the Popeye Suite Puerto Marina for a one-of-a-kind experience, complete with a rooftop pool and beach access.

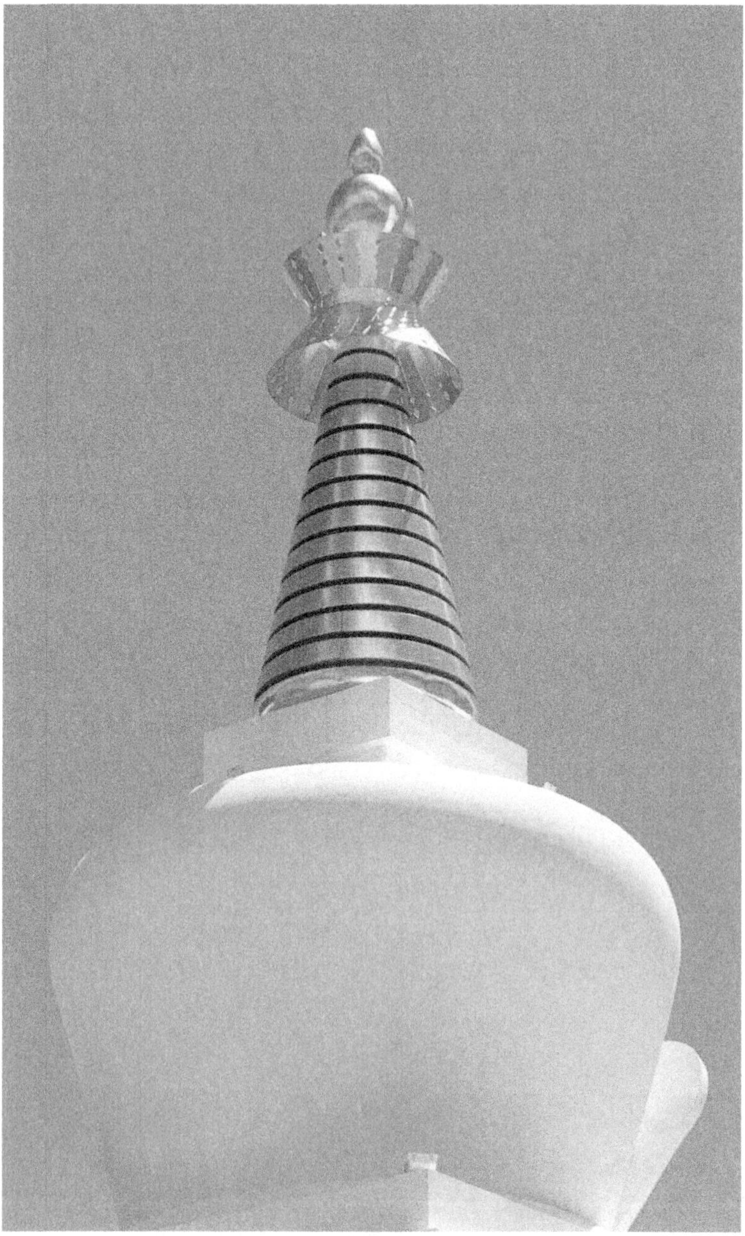

CHAPTER 2

Navigating Benalmádena

Navigating the charming town of Benalmádena is an essential part of your trip. Getting around is both convenient and enjoyable, thanks to the well-organized transportation system and pedestrian-friendly streets. Here's a comprehensive guide to navigating this stunning coastal town with ease.

Getting Around Benalmadena

Benalmádena's small size makes it ideal for exploring on foot, particularly the picturesque Benalmádena Pueblo and the bustling Puerto Marina. For longer distances, the town provides a variety of transportation options:

By Train: The Cercanías train connects Benalmádena to Málaga and nearby coastal towns. The main station, Arroyo de la Miel, is centrally located and offers easy access to numerous attractions.

By Bus: Benalmádena's bus service is reliable and covers most tourist attractions. The buses are frequent, inexpensive, and an excellent way to travel between different parts of the town.

By Taxi: Taxis are easily accessible and can provide a convenient option for direct travel to your destination. They are metered to ensure fair pricing.

By Car: Renting a car allows you to explore at your own pace. If you want to travel outside of Benalmádena, there are several car rental agencies in town.

Car Rentals

Renting a car in Benalmádena allows you to explore at your own pace. There are options for every budget and style, including economy models such as the Fiat 500 and luxury vehicles. You can pick up your rental at Málaga Airport, which is only a short drive from Benalmádena, or at some other locations in town.

Tips for Car Rental

Book in advance, especially during peak seasons, to ensure availability.

Insurance: For added peace of mind, choose comprehensive coverage.

Check the Car: Before driving away, inspect the vehicle for any existing damage.

Best Places to Rent Cars

Rahul Rent a Car

Areas served: Torremolinos and nearby areas

Location: Avenida Antonio Machado, 42, 29631 Benalmádena

Website: https://rahulrentacar.com/

Phone: +34 617 74 94 95

Opening hours: 9:30am–7pm daily.

Good Morning Rent a Car

Areas served: Benalmádena

Location: Av. Antonio Machado, 60, 29630 Málaga

Website: https://goodmorningrentacar.com/

Phone: +34 951 76 87 58

Opening hours: 8am–2pm Monday–Saturday. Closed on Sundays

Malaga U Drive

Areas served: Málaga and nearby areas

Website: http://www.malagaudrive.com/

Phone: +34 602 86 55 41

Opening hours: 8am–11:30pm daily.

Olmedo Rent A Car & Excursions

Areas served: Benalmádena and nearby areas

Location: Avenida Antonio Machado, 42, 29630 Benalmádena

Website: http://www.olmedorentacar.com/

Phone: +34 609 00 17 35

Opening hours: 9:30am–6pm Monday–Friday. 10am–1:30pm Saturday–Sunday.

Transportation Tips

Travel Card: Consider purchasing a local travel card to get cheaper bus and train fares within the Málaga Metropolitan Transport Consortium area.

Trains: Trains are a dependable and time-efficient mode of transportation. Keep your ticket handy because you will need it to get through the turnstiles.

Buses: While buses are slower than trains, they provide a scenic route and connect to destinations not served by rail. Plan your trip ahead of time by checking the schedules.

Taxis: Booking a taxi online can save you time and hassle when traveling to the airport or late at night.

Driving Tips: If you decide to drive, familiarize yourself with local traffic laws. Parking can be difficult during peak season, so make your plans accordingly.

Accessibility:

Benalmádena is committed to accessibility, with most buses and trains designed to accommodate people with mobility issues. Key areas and attractions are also designed to be easily accessible.

Safety and Etiquette:

Safety: Benalmádena is a safe town, but always use common sense, especially at night or in congested areas.

Etiquette: When using public transportation, be respectful of local customs and regulations. Queue politely and offer your seat to someone in need.

Communication and Connectivity

Staying connected in Benalmádena is simple thanks to the city's modern communication infrastructure. Benalmádena's advanced communication and connectivity facilities allow you to enjoy a hassle-free vacation while staying in touch with the world and soaking up the sun and culture of this beautiful Spanish town. Whether you want to share vacation photos, stay in touch with loved ones, or manage work remotely, Benalmádena's connectivity options have you covered.

Internet Access: Benalmádena has high-speed internet, with fiber optic connections readily available, ensuring fast and dependable service for all your online needs. Numerous cafes and restaurants provide free Wi-Fi, allowing you to stay connected while enjoying local cuisine.

Mobile Connectivity: The town is well connected to major mobile networks, which offer excellent 4G and, increasingly, 5G services. This means you can expect high-quality voice calls and fast mobile data services, allowing you to easily navigate, stream, and communicate while exploring.

Broadband providers: Reputable broadband providers provide customized packages for various needs, including basic browsing, high-demand streaming, and gaming. Many providers also provide bilingual customer service, making it easier for international visitors to seek assistance. The main broadband providers in Spain are Movistar, Vodafone, Orange, and MásMóvil.

Communication Tips

SIM Cards: Consider purchasing a local SIM card to get better call and data rates.

When conducting sensitive transactions over public Wi-Fi, always use secure connections.

Language Apps: Use translation apps to remove language barriers and improve your experience.

Basic Communication Words and Pronunciation

Hello - Hola (oh-lah)

Goodbye - Adiós (ah-dee-ohs)

Please - Por favor (por fah-vor)

Thank you - Gracias (grah-see-ahs)

Yes - Sí (see)

No - No (noh)

Excuse me - Perdón (pair-dohn)

Sorry - Lo siento (loh see-en-toh)

How are you? - ¿Cómo estás? (koh-moh ehs-tahs)

I'm fine, thank you - Estoy bien, gracias (ehs-toy byen, grah-see-ahs)

What is your name? - ¿Cómo te llamas? (koh-moh teh yah-mahs)

My name is... - Me llamo... (meh yah-moh)

Where is...? - ¿Dónde está...? (dohn-deh ehs-tah)

How much does it cost? - ¿Cuánto cuesta? (kwan-toh kwehs-tah)

Do you speak English? - ¿Hablas inglés? (ah-blahs een-glehs)

I don't understand - No entiendo (noh ehn-tyen-doh)

Can you help me? - ¿Puedes ayudarme? (pweh-dehs ah-yoo-dar-meh)

Bathroom - Baño (bah-nyoh)

Restaurant - Restaurante (rehs-tow-rahn-teh)

Hotel - Hotel (oh-tehl)

Taxi - Taxi (tahk-see)

Bus - Autobús (ow-toh-boos)

Train - Tren (trehn)

Airport - Aeropuerto (ah-eh-roh-pwehr-toh)

Street - Calle (kah-yeh)

Left - Izquierda (ees-kyehr-dah)

Right - Derecha (deh-reh-chah)

Straight - Recto (rehk-toh)

Stop - Parada (pah-rah-dah)

Open - Abierto (ah-byehr-toh)

Closed - Cerrado (sehr-rah-doh)

Entrance - Entrada (ehn-trah-dah)

Exit - Salida (sah-lee-dah)

Help - Ayuda (ah-yoo-dah)

Police - Policía (poh-lee-see-ah)

Hospital - Hospital (ohs-pee-tahl)

Doctor - Médico (meh-dee-koh)

Pharmacy - Farmacia (fahr-mah-see-ah)

Numbers:

One - Uno (oo-noh)

Two - Dos (dohs)

Three - Tres (trehs)

Four - Cuatro (kwah-troh)

Five - Cinco (seen-koh)

Six - Seis (says)

Seven - Siete (syeh-teh)

Eight - Ocho (oh-cho)

Nine - Nueve (nweh-veh)

Ten - Diez (dyehs)

What time is it? - ¿Qué hora es? (keh oh-rah ehs)

Can you recommend a good restaurant? - ¿Puedes recomendar un buen restaurante? (pweh-dehs reh-koh-mehn-dar oon bwehn rehs-tow-rahn-teh)

Where can I find a map? - ¿Dónde puedo encontrar un mapa? (dohn-deh pweh-doh ehn-kon-trar oon mah-pah)

How can I get to...? - ¿Cómo puedo llegar a...? (koh-moh pweh-doh yeh-gar ah)

Can I pay with a credit card? - ¿Puedo pagar con tarjeta de crédito? (pweh-doh pah-gar kon tar-heh-tah deh kre-dee-toh)

Is there Wi-Fi here? - ¿Hay Wi-Fi aquí? (ay wee-fee ah-kee)

What is the weather like today? - ¿Cómo está el tiempo hoy? (koh-moh ehs-tah ehl tee-ehm-poh oy)

Where can I buy souvenirs? - ¿Dónde puedo comprar recuerdos? (dohn-deh pweh-doh kom-prar reh-kwehr-dohs)

Can I have the bill, please? - ¿Me trae la cuenta, por favor? (meh trah-eh lah kwehn-tah por fah-vor)

I need a reservation for... - Necesito una reserva para... (neh-seh-see-toh oo-nah reh-sehr-bah pah-rah)

Can you call a taxi for me? - ¿Puedes llamar a un taxi para mí? (pweh-dehs yah-mahr ah oon tahk-see pah-rah mee)

Can you show me on the map? - ¿Puedes mostrarme en el mapa? (pweh-dehs moh-strar-meh en el mah-pah)

I'm lost - Estoy perdido/perdida (ehs-toy pair-dee-doh/pair-dee-dah)

What time does it open/close? - ¿A qué hora abre/cierra? (ah keh oh-rah ah-breh/syeh-rah)

Do you have a menu in English? - ¿Tienes un menú en inglés? (tyeh-nes oon meh-noo en een-gles)

Is there a public restroom nearby? - ¿Hay un baño público cerca? (ay oon bah-nyoh poo-blee-koh sehr-kah)

Can you take a photo of us, please? - ¿Puedes hacernos una foto, por favor? (pweh-dehs ah-sehr-nohs oo-nah fo-toh por fah-vor)

How far is it to...? - ¿Qué tan lejos está...? (keh tan leh-hos ehs-tah)

Can you recommend any local attractions? - ¿Puedes recomendar algunas atracciones locales? (pweh-dehs reh-koh-mehn-dar ah-goo-nahs ah-trahk-syoh-nes loh-kah-les)

Is there a bank nearby? - ¿Hay un banco cercano? (ay oon bahn-koh sehr-kah-noh)

Can you speak slower, please? - ¿Puedes hablar más despacio, por favor? (pweh-dehs ah-blar mahs dehs-pah-syo por fah-vor)

Currency, Cards, Tipping and Tax Information

Navigating the financial aspects of your Benalmádena adventure is critical to a smooth experience. Understanding these financial essentials will allow you to enjoy the beautiful sights and experiences Benalmádena has to offer without any financial surprises. Here's a tourist-friendly guide to currency, credit card usage, tipping, and taxes.

Currency: Benalmádena, like the rest of Spain, uses the Euro as its official currency. Local exchange offices provide competitive rates for currency exchange services, making them easily accessible. For convenience, it is recommended that you exchange some money before your arrival.

Cards: Credit and debit cards are commonly accepted in Benalmádena, especially Visa and MasterCard. Card payments have recently become the norm in many establishments, including smaller venues. However, it is always a good idea to carry some cash for places that do not accept cards or for small purchases where cards may incur additional fees.

Tipping: Tipping is optional in Benalmádena, but it is seen as a sign of appreciation for the service provided. If you are satisfied with the service at a restaurant, bar, or cafe, it is customary to leave a tip of 5-10% of the total bill. For taxi drivers, rounding up the fare or adding a euro or two is a common practice. Hotel employees, such as cleaners and porters, appreciate a small tip for excellent service.

Tax: Spain has a Value Added Tax (VAT) called IVA, which is included in the price of most goods and services. As a tourist, you may be able to claim a tax refund on purchases made during your stay. Keep your receipts and look for the Tax-Free Shopping sign in stores to take advantage of this benefit. There is no specific tourist tax in Benalmádena, so you won't have to worry about any additional fees upon arrival.

How to Save Money in Benalmádena

Saving money in Benalmádena entails careful planning and taking advantage of the town's numerous free or low-cost attractions. Here are some tips for enjoying your stay without overspending:

Take Advantage of Free Attractions: Explore Benalmádena Pueblo's rich cultural heritage or stroll along the picturesque Paseo Maritimo. Both provide delightful experiences at no cost.

Visit Paloma Park: Relax in the lush greenery of Paloma Park, where you can enjoy a picnic and the company of friendly animals, all for free.

Sunset Views: Find a hill in town and watch the stunning sunset over the lake, a great way to end your day without spending a dime.

Affordable Eats: Indulge in local cuisine at a reasonable price. Look for restaurants that serve tapas and drinks at low prices.

Public Transport: Rather than renting a car or taking a taxi, use the efficient public transportation system to get around.

Accommodation: Look for low-cost options or book ahead of time during the off-season for better deals.

Useful Apps and Resources

These apps cover all aspects of travel, from planning and booking to navigation and communication, ensuring a smooth and enjoyable experience in Benalmádena.

Skyscanner: To find the best flights to Benalmádena.

GetYourGuide: Book tours and learn about Benalmádena's popular attractions.

Google Maps: A must-have app for navigation, finding places of interest, and figuring out transit routes.

Consorco Malaga: The best app for finding the most recent bus and train schedules in Benalmádena. This app provides timetables, routes, and updates for all local transportation services in the area. It is available on iTunes and Google Play, making it accessible to most smartphone users.

XE Currency: Useful for currency conversions to help you manage your travel budget efficiently.

Google Translate: Uses text and voice translations to help people communicate across languages.

Uber: Easy to book rides if you need quick and dependable transportation.

WeatherPro: Get detailed weather forecasts to help you plan your daily activities.

WhatsApp: Popular for free messaging and calls, it's ideal for staying in touch with locals or other travelers.

SpanishDict: A Spanish-English dictionary app designed for quick translations and learning common phrases.

Booking.com: This hotel booking app allows you to search, compare, and book hotels in Benalmádena and Spain. You can use it to find the best prices, reviews, and availability for your lodging needs.

TripIt: You can save all your trip documents, flights, car rentals, hotels, and activities in the TripIt app. In addition, the app will notify you if there are any changes to your flight or vacation information. It will even notify you when it is time to go to the airport.

Duolingo: If you want to learn some basic Spanish phrases before your vacation, Duolingo is the perfect tool for you. Get the app to play entertaining language games, learn some essential travel words, and get a sense of how Spanish sounds.

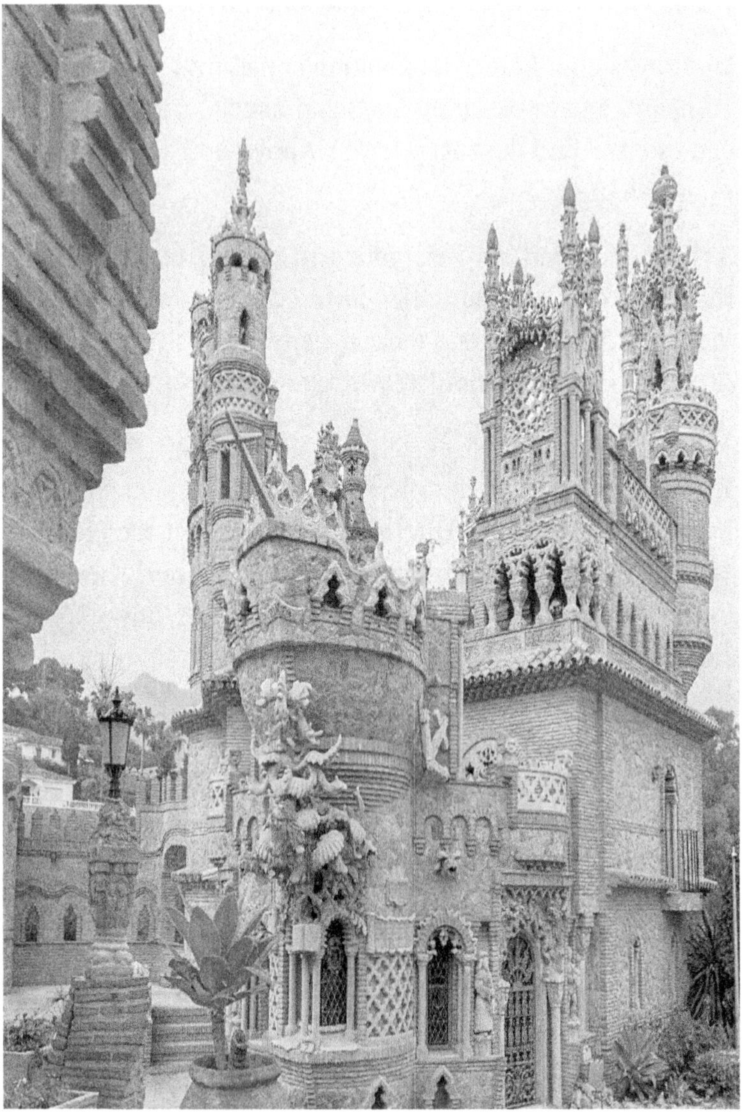

CHAPTER 3

Where to Stay

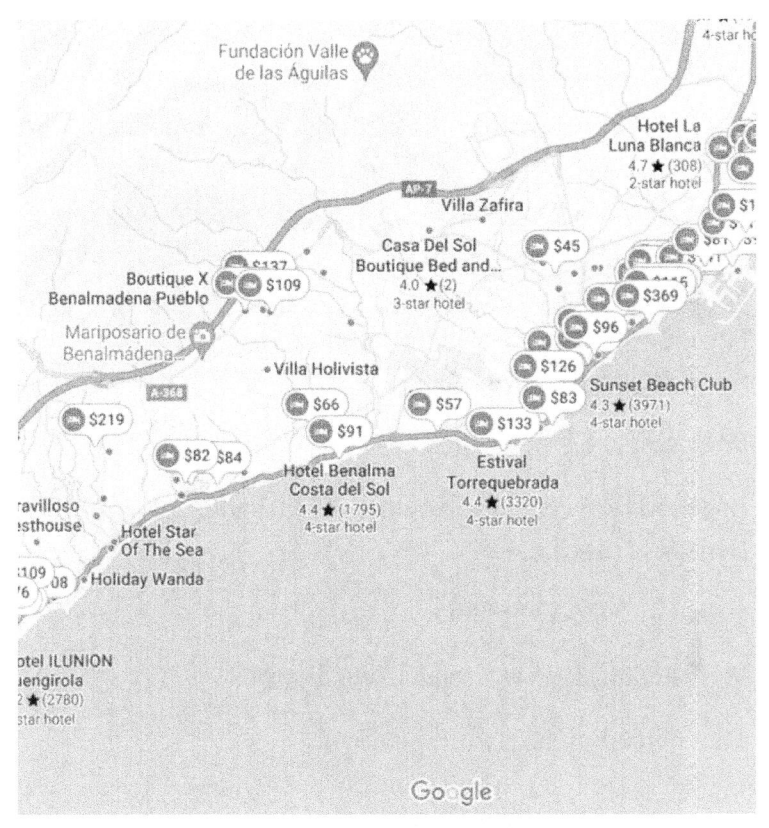

https://maps.app.goo.gl/2thW2EmgG9gEYDqD7

Benalmádena has a wide range of accommodations to suit every preference and budget. Whether you want luxury, affordability, uniqueness, or romance, this guide will help you find the ideal place to stay. Each of these accommodations offers a unique experience, ensuring that your time in Benalmádena is as memorable as the town itself.

Luxury Stays

Vincci Selección Aleysa Hotel

This elegant beachfront hotel provides an intimate setting with breathtaking sea views, an outdoor pool, and a hot tub. The hotel is immaculately clean and well-decorated. The personnel are pleasant and eager to go above and above to ensure your stay is as enjoyable as possible. The rooms are big and equipped with all the necessary amenities. They also serve great a la carte dishes.

Price range: $215 - $636

Location: Avenida Antonio Machado, 57, 29630 Benalmádena

Phone: (+34) 952 566566

Website: https://www.vinccialeysa.com/

Map Direction: https://rb.gy/qlyvqr

Hotel Mac Puerto Marina Benalmádena

Adjacent to the lively marina, this hotel has an outdoor pool and rooms with balconies or terraces. It is a wonderful location near the street and beach, and they provide wonderful service, and very delicious meals at the restaurant, the Spa is fantastic, and the bar personnel are extremely kind and helpful.

Price range: $123 - $216

Location: Avenida del Puerto Deportivo S/N, 29630, Benalmádena

Phone: +34 952 961 696

Website: https://www.macpuertomarina.com/

Map Direction: https://rb.gy/q3l5r8

Sunset Beach Club

These apartments feature two outdoor pools, and six seasonal bars and restaurants, and provide a self-contained luxury experience. The location, facilities, room quality, neatness, and convenience are excellent. The beds are quite comfortable. The employees are professional and helpful. There is a small kitchen in the apartment. The resort's small market provides an excellent assortment of products at reasonable costs.

Price range: $88 - $134

Location: Avenida del Sol, 5, 29630 Benalmádena

Phone: +34 952 579 400

Website: http://www.sunsetbeachclub.com/

Map Direction: https://rb.gy/t1u31h

Estival Torrequebrada

With sea views from every room, this hotel features indoor and outdoor pools, a casino, and a buffet restaurant. The hotel is near the beach, and there are several restaurants and stores in the vicinity. There is also a casino if you want to have some fun. The staff is nice and diligent, and the standard of cleanliness is superb. The meal was delicious. Towels are also replaced every day.

Price range: $89 - $153

Location: Avenida del Sol, 89, 29630 Benalmádena

Phone: +34 952 579 500

Website: https://estivaltorrequebrada.com/

Map Direction: https://rb.gy/wo3apo

Hotel Best Siroco

Located near Torre Bermeja Beach, this hotel is known for its affordability and romantic atmosphere. Great location, just a few minutes' walk from the Marina and promenade. The yard is beautiful, the rooms are comfortable, and the pools are great for relaxing. Good food and excellent service at the restaurant. The bartenders are also amazing.

Price range: $93 - $147

Location: Carril del Siroco, S/N, 29630 Benalmádena

Phone: +34 952 443 040

Map Direction: https://rb.gy/ux78mc

Budget-Friendly Stays

Hostal Sol y Miel

This charming hostel provides free high-speed WiFi and rooms with private bathrooms and flat-screen televisions. It is close to the station and convenient for stores and eateries. Perfectly clean, comfortable mattresses, powerful shower, and kind personnel. Some rooms feature balconies from which to observe the outside world go by.

Price range: $51 - $75

Location: Avenida Blas Infante, 14, 29631 Benalmádena

Phone: +34 951 204 440

Website: http://www.solymiel.com/

Map Direction: https://rb.gy/mpq353

Hotel Betania

An affordable option with basic amenities and a convenient location. The rooms are ensuite, and the location is ideal for getting around town and doing activities you enjoy. The beds are excellent, however, there is no air conditioning in the room. Friendly and helpful staff.

Price range: $39 - $63

Location: Calle Carril de Contreras 12, Benalmádena

Phone: +34 952 577 786

Website: https://www.hotelbetania.es/

Map Direction: https://rb.gy/duqpn1

Boutique Hotel Pueblo

A boutique guest house located in the traditional white village, with scenic views and a welcoming atmosphere. A lovely hotel in a good, central location. Susanne, the owner, is incredibly pleasant and helpful. The rooms are tidy and comfortable.

Price range: $78 - $90

Location: Avenida Juan Luis Peralta, S/N, 29639 Benalmádena

Phone: +34 603 11 12 91

Website: https://hotelpueblo.es/

Map Direction: https://rb.gy/4fl77n

Apartamentos MS Pepita

Apartments near the marina offer a comfortable stay with kitchenettes and balconies. The location is ideal for promenade walks, with easy access to the major bus route and a short stroll to the harbor. The flat is spacious, tidy, and well-equipped. The staff are kind and helpful.

Price range: $63 - $103

Location: Avenida Alay, 1, 29630 Benalmádena

Phone: +34 952 560 100

Website: http://www.apartamentosmsalay.com/

Map Direction: https://rb.gy/e53iat

Sahara Sunset

Very inviting, and the bed is comfortable. Everything is nearby, including the beach, and there are beautiful walks up to the marina or Arroyo. The Casbah is a nice on-site restaurant with great food, reasonable pricing, and fantastic personnel. It also has a mini supermarket.

Price range: $103 - $195

Location: Avenida Rocío Jurado, S/N, 29630 Benalmádena

Phone: +34 952 440 258

Website: https://rb.gy/ryv5os

Map Direction: https://rb.gy/aeocdx

Unique Stays

Holiday World Polynesia Hotel

Great hotel with delicious meals, and the staff is always willing to help. The rooms are wonderful, large, and cleaned every day. The spa is also excellent. Wonderful snack/meal with lots of variety. The hotel provides all you need for a brief stay. There is an extra fee for the wristbands for the bowling, arcades, and spa, refundable upon checkout.

Price range: $85 - $222

Location: Rotonda de los Elefantes, Av. del Sol, 195, 29630 Benalmádena

Phone: +34 952 57 97 57

Website: https://rb.gy/6rpl3h

Map Direction: https://rb.gy/fwjvpv

Hotel SPA Benalmádena Palace

Nice hotel with an indoor pool in a convenient location. Well-equipped, large, and clean apartments, with a buffet-style breakfast with many options. The hotel is fully equipped for families. The staff are polite and professional.

Price range: $98 - $162

Location: Camino Gilabert, S/N, 29630 Benalmádena

Phone: +34 952 96 49 58

Website: https://rb.gy/yvwkpf

Map Direction: https://rb.gy/y98xof

Finca La Vida Loca B&B (Adults Only)

This boutique B&B boasts stunning interior design and breathtaking sea views. Willem and Teddy have done an excellent job with this boutique B&B. The rooms are tastefully designed and cleaned every day, so they are sparkling. The pool area is like a gorgeous paradise with trees and flowers. It is also quite peaceful. The hosts, Teddy and Willem, are helpful and make you feel at home. The breakfast is delicious and plentiful.

Price range: $162 - $345

Location: Address: Camino. del Amocafre, s/n, 29639 Benalmádena

Phone: +32 476 252 545

Website: https://fincalavidaloca.com/en/the-environment/

Map Direction: https://rb.gy/rnyidn

Hotel Las Arenas, Affiliated By Meliá

This Hotel provides a range of amenities including sea views, a pool, a jacuzzi, and free Wi-Fi. The hotel's prime position, facing the sea and Bil Bil Castle, makes it a popular choice for both sunbathers and those interested in local culture. Guests will have a comfortable stay with functional furnishings and a bathroom with a bathtub in their rooms. The hotel is also known for its buffet restaurant and outdoor pool, and it is conveniently located near Black Jack Sports & Family Bar and Scanlon's Shamrock Bar.

Price range: $140 - $198

Location: Avenida Antonio Machado, 122, 29630 Benalmádena

Phone: +34 952 44 36 44

Website: https://rb.gy/ueb048

Map Direction: https://rb.gy/wmldfn

Hotel Benalma Costa del Sol

This is a beautiful hotel in one of the calmer neighborhoods that views directly out to the sea. The rooms are big and well-equipped, with a safe provided at no additional cost. The meal is superb, with a large selection to pick from, and all wine is served in bottles rather than dispensers. Benalma has an excellent staff. Public transportation, including buses and trains, is within walking distance.

Price range: $94 - $180

Location: N-340, km 217, 29630 Benalmádena

Phone: +34 952 56 95 12

Website: https://rb.gy/1ynvp5

Map Direction: https://rb.gy/7uyjl8

Romantic Stays

Boutique Hotel Pueblo

A boutique guest house located in the traditional white village, with scenic views and a welcoming atmosphere. A lovely hotel in a good, central location. Susanne, the owner, is incredibly pleasant and helpful. The rooms are tidy and comfortable.

Price range: $78 - $90

Location: Avenida Juan Luis Peralta, S/N, 29639 Benalmádena

Phone: +34 603 11 12 91

Website: https://hotelpueblo.es/

Map Direction: https://rb.gy/4f177n

Hotel Casa Rosa

A family-run hotel in the town center with bright, air-conditioned rooms and beautiful sea views. A wonderful, clean, and large room. The rooms are nicely designed and immaculately clean. The staff is courteous and always willing to help. Breakfast is a must-do experience; it is handmade and couldn't be more fresh.

Price range: $65 - $92

Location: Address: Camino. Pensamiento, 31, 29639 Benalmádena

Phone: +32 952 568 047

Website: https://www.hotelcasarosabenalmadena.com/en/

Map Direction: https://rb.gy/af3xga

Hotel La Fonda

This beautifully restored white building features an outdoor swimming pool and a traditional Andalusian internal patio. Very clean, nice accommodations, and excellent service. Breakfast options are fantastic. There are also other excellent pubs and tapas restaurants nearby. The hotel boasts an incredible swimming pool located in the heart of the property.

Price range: $109 - $151

Location: de Guzmán, C. Santo Domingo, 7, 29639 Benalmádena

Phone: +34 952 569 047

Website: http://www.lafondabenalmadena.es/

Map Direction: https://rb.gy/x2hrrx

Hotel Mac Puerto Marina Benalmádena

Adjacent to the lively marina, this hotel has an outdoor pool and rooms with balconies or terraces. It is a wonderful location near the street and beach, and they provide wonderful service, and very delicious meals at the restaurant, the Spa is fantastic, and the bar personnel are extremely kind and helpful.

Price range: $123 - $216

Location: Avenida del Puerto Deportivo S/N, 29630, Benalmádena

Phone: +34 952 961 696

Website: https://www.macpuertomarina.com/

Map Direction: https://rb.gy/q3l5r8

Royal Oasis Club at Pueblo Quinta

Provides a tranquil retreat with well-appointed apartments and access to a variety of recreational amenities. A very tidy hotel, conveniently placed near several lovely cities, shopping malls, restaurants, and beaches. Royal Oasis Club's personnel are courteous and helpful. Price range: $93 - $155

Location: Urbanización Pueblo Quinta, Avenida Federico García Lorca, 8, 29630 Benalmádena

Phone: +34 952 563 479

Booking: https://rb.gy/ddm6ch

Map Direction: https://rb.gy/fzja27

CHAPTER 4

Discover Benalmádena Wonders

Explore the charms of Benalmádena, a coastal town full of beauty and adventure. Whether you are looking for exciting activities, cultural experiences, or hidden gems, this guide will take you right to the heart of Benalmádena's charm.

Things To Do

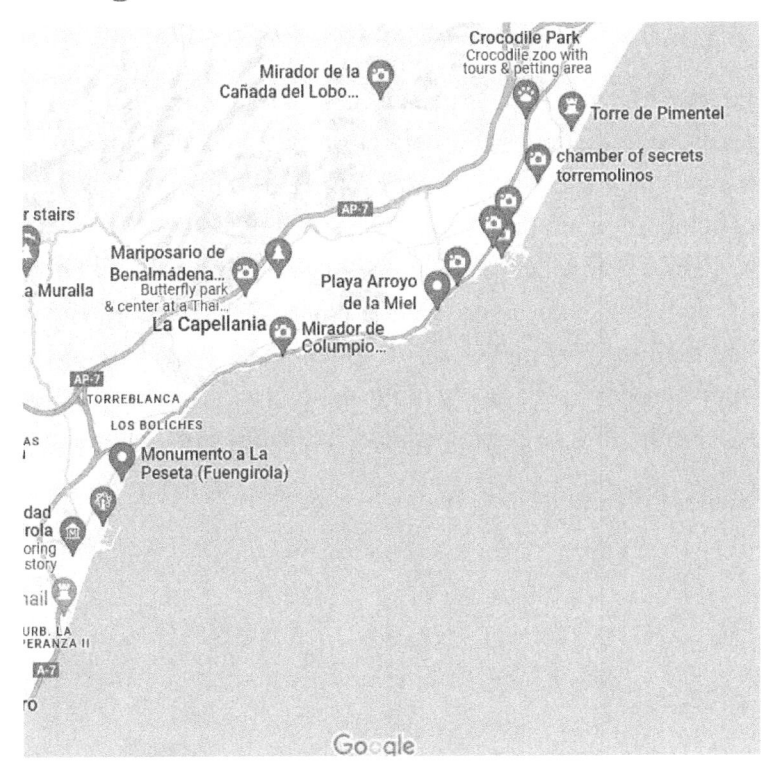

https://maps.app.goo.gl/rDcow6mXmf2EbRCZA

Benalmádena is a playground for all ages. Stroll along the Paseo Maritimo, a promenade packed with cafes and stores, or engage in water sports on the beach. Enjoy a fun-filled day with the family at Sea Life Benalmádena's vivid marine life or Tivoli World, an amusement park featuring rides and entertainment.

Top Attractions:

Puerto Marina Benalmadena

Puerto Marina Benalmadena is a world-class marina, it features a distinctive architectural design and has been named the Best Marina in the World several times. It was officially opened in 1979 and was previously known as Port au Prince before being renamed in 1982. The marina is a hive of activity, with over 1,000 docks for boats of many nationalities, a plethora of fine restaurants, shopping opportunities, and a lively nightlife. It is an ideal location for tourists to go for relaxing walks, eat, shop, and have fun.

Map Direction: https://rb.gy/hz3x2p

Benalmadena Pueblo (the Old Village)

It is a classic Andalusian village with narrow streets, whitewashed houses, a fascinating history, and lots of lovely spots to eat. A typical Spanish town, with small shops and narrow streets. There are several good restaurants and attractions around. Begin your trip at the central Plaza de Espana, where you can shop for local crafts and try some tapas and wine. It is near the coast yet far from the tourist traps. It contains several secret plazas. You must walk around to discover these hidden gems. A lovely church, a Buddhist temple, and El Muro Gardens, which offer panoramic views, are among the top attractions. The village has a lift for easy access between its levels. Be on the lookout for incoming vehicles as cars still pass by despite that the streets are small.

Map Direction: https://rb.gy/n4mxgv

Plaza Espana

Plaza de España is a bustling hub that represents the spirit of Spanish culture. A lovely square surrounded by classic, white-washed buildings in the heart of Benalmádena Pueblo. The plaza features the famous sculpture Niña de Benalmádena, a symbol of the town. You can enjoy Spanish foods at local eateries, relax by the lovely fountain, or immerse yourself in the peaceful ambiance. It's an ideal location to enjoy the elegance of Andalusian life and a must-see for anyone visiting the old village. It's a great area to take shelter from the sun in the summer and decide the next thing to do.

Map Direction: https://rb.gy/dsk92s

Parque De La Paloma

It is a lovely refuge that covers more than 200,000 square meters and features an artificial lake, a variety of wildlife, and lush gardens. You can stroll along its paved pathways, relax by the lake, or enjoy the playgrounds. The park is home to a variety of animals, including peacocks and rabbits that roam freely. It's ideal for families, nature enthusiasts, and anyone wishing to relax surrounded by greenery and fresh air. The park's central location makes it a readily accessible and must-see attraction.

Location: Avenida Federico García Lorca, s/n, 29630 Benalmádena.

Map Direction: https://rb.gy/fve7hr

Open every day from 9 a.m. to 11 p.m.

Teleferico de Benalmadena

Teleferico Benalmadena, also known as the Benalmadena Cable Car, provides a spectacular aerial journey from the coastal town to the top of Monte Calamorro. It offers breathtaking panoramic views of the Costa del Sol and, on clear days, Gibraltar and the African coast. You can enjoy falconry exhibitions, hiking routes, and the beautiful

Mediterranean flora at the top. The cable car operates daily and provides an audio tour to enhance the experience. It's a must-see for stunning views and a sense of adventure in the heart of Benalmádena. If you want to enjoy some breathtaking views without any hassle, take a Cable Car to Mount Calamoro. Tickets start at 12 euros online and cost 18 euros on the spot. Purchase online at https://rb.gy/mrlu88

Website: https://www.telefericobenalmadena.com/en

Location: Explanada del Tivoli, s/n, 29631 Benalmádena

Map Direction: https://rb.gy/v2d1zd

Open every day from 11 a.m. to 7 p.m.

Butterfly Park, Benalmadena

The Butterfly Park of Benalmadena is a tropical paradise where tourists can see over 1,500 species of butterflies from all over the world. The park, which is next to the Buddhist Stupa, has waterfalls and flowers in an atmosphere reminiscent of a Thai temple. It's the biggest butterfly park in Europe and provides educational insights into the butterfly's life cycle. There is a small enclosure for other greenhouse dwellers, a souvenir shop, a cafeteria, and a butterfly nursery where you can watch the butterflies hatch. It is a calm place where you can see these delicate creatures take their maiden flight and get up close and personal with them in their natural habitat, it's open every day. Purchase tickets online for 10.50 euros per person at https://www.mariposariodebenalmadena.com/tienda/

Location: C. Muerdago, S/N, 29639 Benalmádena.

Map Direction: https://rb.gy/walkve

Open every day from 10 a.m. to 7.30 p.m.

Castillo de Colomares

Castillo de Colomares is a unique monument dedicated to Christopher Columbus and his voyages. Constructed between 1987 and 1994, it is notable for its elaborate design that combines numerous architectural styles to tell the story of the Discovery of America. The castle-like edifice also has one of the world's tiniest churches. In addition to learning about the historical voyage to the New World, you can admire the replicas of Columbus's ships, the Niña, Pinta, and Santa María. It's an incredible site for photography and views, and even children will enjoy running around and exploring the water features. They have a small café and restrooms on-site. It is a remarkable site that combines history, art, and architecture, open all year except Mondays. Purchase tickets at the counter at the entrance. It costs 3 euros per adult and 2 euros per child.

Website: https://www.castillomonumentocolomares.com/

Location: Finca la Carraca, Ctra Costa del Sol, s/n, 29639 Benalmádena.

Map Direction: https://rb.gy/nsekhz

Opening hours: check the schedule section of the website.

Selwo Marina

Selwo Marina is a marine park that provides close encounters with many marine species. It offers interactive events such as dolphin shows, swimming with sea lions, and penguin feedings. The park is separated into zones, such as Antillas, Amazonia, Las Hondonada, and Isla de Hielo, each with a different species. Tourists can attend informative seminars and demonstrations that emphasize the importance of conservation. It is a family-friendly destination that allows visitors to learn about and engage with the aquatic world.

Website: https://www.selwomarina.es/en

Location: Parque de la Paloma s/n, 29630 Benalmádena

Map Direction: https://rb.gy/sjj25u

Open every day from 10 a.m. to 6 p.m.

Bil-Bil Castle (Castillo de El-Bil-Bil)

Bil-Bil Castle is a prominent landmark with a vivid crimson facade and Arabic-style architecture. Built in 1927, it was used as a private residence before being bought by the town council in 1980. Today, it serves as a cultural center, for hosting weddings, concerts, and exhibitions. Its prime location on the beachfront makes it an appealing destination for visitors. Beautiful gardens and nighttime illumination are other highlights of the castle. It is open to the public and worth a visit for its historical significance and breathtaking views.

Website: https://rb.gy/9x8stn

Location: Av. Antonio Machado 78, 29631 Benalmádena.

Map Direction: https://rb.gy/yx9suy

Opening Hours: check the website for up-to-date opening hours.

Stupa of Enlightenment in Benalmádena

The Stupa of Enlightenment represents tranquility and meditation. With its impressive 33-meter height, this stupa is the tallest in Europe and provides breathtaking views of the Costa del Sol. It was inaugurated on October 5, 2003, and inspired by Buddhist Master Lopon Tsechu Rinpoche. The stupa is distinguished by its meditation hall and serves as a space for introspection and learning about Buddhist teachings. It is handled by the Asociación Cultural Karma Kagyu de Benalmádena, which is led by the 17th Gyalwa

Karmapa, Trinley Thaye Dorje. A little playground and car park are conveniently located close to the temple.

Website: https://www.stupabenalmadena.org/en/

Location: El Retamar, 29639 Benalmádena Pueblo

Map Direction: https://rb.gy/9umrlt

Opening hours: Tuesday through Sunday from 10 am to 2 pm and 4 pm to 6:30 pm. Closed on Mondays

Sea Life Benalmádena

Sea Life Benalmádena is a lively aquarium located in the center of Benalmádena's Puerto Marina. It features over 5,000 aquatic creatures including sharks, rays, and Yellow, a green turtle. The aquarium provides engaging activities, such as touch pools and feeding displays, with an emphasis on education and conservation. It is a family-friendly attraction that gives visitors a glimpse into the undersea world with its bioluminescent experience and daily creature feedings. Sea Life Benalmádena is a must-see for ocean lovers and anyone interested in marine biodiversity. It is open every day. Tickets start at 19.50 euros. Purchase your tickets at: https://www.visitsealife.com/benalmadena/en/tickets/

Location: Av. del Puerto Deportivo, S/N, 29630 Benalmádena.

Map Direction: https://rb.gy/e55y7e

Opening hours: 11 am to 7 pm daily

Garden of Eagles

The Garden of Eagles, also known as Jardin de Las Aguilas, is a mesmerizing Birds of Prey attraction in Benalmádena. Situated atop Mount Calamorro, it provides an opportunity for guests to witness the flying displays of magnificent raptors, such as falcons, eagles, and hawks. In addition to offering an exciting and informative experience, the facility is committed to the breeding and preservation of these species. The facility houses more than 160 bird species, including some rare ones, such as the condor. It is open daily, and the cable car ride to the summit adds to the adventure by providing panoramic views of the Mediterranean.

Map Direction: https://rb.gy/gf1qbw

Open Hours: check https://rb.gy/ce5mzc for updated hours.

Malapesquera Beach

Malapesquera Beach is a famous Benalmádena attraction with a Blue Flag rating, which indicates good environmental and quality standards. The beach spans 700 meters (about 2296.59 ft) and features a vast expanse of sand and mild waves perfect for swimming and sunbathing. Sunbeds and parasols are available, and guests can quench their thirst at one of the many chiringuitos (beach bars) in the area. It is conveniently located near Puerto Marina and is ideal for a relaxed day by the Mediterranean Sea.

Map Direction: https://rb.gy/q1vjs9

Golf Torrequebrada

Golf Torrequebrada, located in the heart of the Costa del Sol, is a gorgeous golf course created by José Pepe Gancedo, also known as the Picasso of golf. It was established in 1976 and provides a delightful 18-hole experience for golfers of all skill levels. The course is known for its strategic bunkers, wide undulating greens, and picturesque fairways flanked with palm trees, pines, and olive trees. Visit the website to make your reservations.

Website: https://golftorrequebrada.com/

Location: Calle Club de Golf, 1. Torrequebrada Urbanization

29630 Benalmádena

Map Direction: https://rb.gy/iemjl9

Open Hours: 7.30 am to 8 pm daily.

Culture House Benalmádena (Casa de la Cultura)

The Culture House of Benalmadena, also known as Casa de la Cultura, is a significant municipal building rooted in the history and tradition of the town. It stands out for its architectural beauty and serves as the center for cultural activities and Town Hall events. It is the focal point of Arroyo de la Miel, located on Avenida de la Constitución, Plaza de Austria. The Culture House hosts various events, from art exhibitions to performances, making it a cultural hub for locals and tourists.

Location: Plaza Austria, s/n, 29631 Arroyo De La Miel-Benalmádena

Map Direction: https://rb.gy/vbc4k4

Open Hours: Monday to Friday from 9 am–1 pm and 4 pm – 10 pm.

Playa Arroyo de La Miel

Playa Arroyo de la Miel is a beautiful beach recognized for its great facilities and calm waters. The location is easily accessible via the lovely Paseo Marítimo and flanked by enticing chiringuitos. The beach is perfect for swimming and relaxing as it is well-maintained, has clean sand, and has a serene ambiance. It's also family-friendly, with gentle waves and a reputation for safety. You can enjoy the sun, sea, and a variety of beach activities, providing a pleasant stay on the Costa del Sol.

Map Direction: https://rb.gy/drwail

6 Hidden Gems for the Adventurous Souls:

Molino de Inca Botanical Garden

Visit the Botanical Garden, a lovely botanical garden located outside of Benalmadena. The botanical garden and museum at Molino de Inca, in the neighboring town of Torremolinos, are a great place to learn about the city's history and its lovely surroundings. The museum is housed in a rebuilt mill. Adult tickets are 3 euros, 1 euro for locals, and free for children under the age of six.

Website: https://turismotorremolinos.es/en/discover/places-of-interest/molino-inca/

Location: Cam. de los Pinares, 29620 Torremolinos

Map Direction: https://rb.gy/oqmb31

Opening hours: Tuesday to Sunday from 10 am to 6 pm

Prison Island

Prison Island is a thrilling adventure park with a unique combination of escape room puzzles and physical activities. It was inspired by television shows such as Fort Boyard and Crystal Maze, in which collaboration is required to solve puzzles and win points. The park has 24 cells with varied tasks to test your ability, strength, and intellect. It is appropriate for all ages, making it an excellent choice for families, friends, and team-building activities. Prison Island is open every day and offers a fun and competitive setting for tourists to enjoy.

Website: https://www.prisonisland.es/en/

Location: Puerto Marina Shopping, Plaza de la Goleta s/n C.C, Local L3, 29631 Benalmádena

Map Direction: https://rb.gy/0ace9q

Open Hours: 10 am – 9 pm daily.

Carvajal Beach

Carvajal Beach is a tranquil and gorgeous beach on the outskirts of Fuengirola that smoothly blends into Benalmádena Costa. It is renowned for its excellent chiringuitos (beach bars) and fantastic beach quality. With no road access, it provides a safer atmosphere, particularly for youngsters. The beach is easily accessible from the Paseo Maritimo Rey De España. It is a quieter option compared to other nearby beaches, great for those wanting relaxation away from the crowds.

Map Direction: https://rb.gy/6rg3eo

Playa de Benalnatura

Playa de Benalnatura is a secluded naturist beach in Benalmádena, known for its privacy and natural beauty. It is one of the few nudist beaches on the Costa del Sol, located in a cove surrounded by rocks. Entrance is via a stairway that leads to a beach bar; guests must be at least eighteen and not wearing clothing to enter. The tranquil sea is great for swimming and snorkeling due to its clean water and serene setting. Remember to bring sun umbrellas and chairs, as services are limited. It is an ideal location for anyone wanting a naturalist experience.

Map Direction: https://rb.gy/kzfjf7

Benalmádena Museum

Benalmádena Museum, also known as the Felipe Orlando Museum, is a cultural gem situated in the old town area of Benalmádena. It was founded in 1970 and renovated in 2005 and now holds one of the biggest collections of pre-Columbian art outside of Hispanic America. The museum's archeological collection ranges from ancient origins to Ancient Rome, highlighting the region's rich past. It is open from Tuesday to Sunday and allows visitors to discover history via exciting exhibits and educational events.

Website: https://rb.gy/occnio

Location: Plaza de las Tres Culturas, 29639 Benalmádena

Map Direction: https://rb.gy/etno0n

Opening Hours: check the website for up-to-date opening hours.

Santo Domingo Church (Iglesia de Santo Domingo de Guzmán)

The Iglesia de Santo Domingo de Guzmán is a historical church constructed in the 17th century and situated in a small garden in Benalmadena's Old Town. It is the town's oldest church and is believed to have been built on the site of a medieval temple near the ancient defensive wall. The church, located in Plaza Santo Domingo, the town's original center, it has a bulrush belfry with three bells and a clock. It has undergone many modifications, the most recent in 1998. On clear days, the church grounds provide a panoramic view of the city and the sea, as well as the North African coastline.

Location: C. Santo Domingo, 16, 29639 Benalmádena.

Map Direction: https://rb.gy/opc2s5

Cultural Experiences and Shows

The rich history and sophisticated edge of Benalmádena are reflected in the town's lively cultural landscape. Here's an overview of the cultural performances and shows that tourists can enjoy:

Flamenco Benalmádena

Flamenco Benalmadena is a lively celebration of true flamenco that captures the essence of traditional Spanish culture. It offers guests the opportunity to witness the passionate dancing and music that are intrinsic to Andalusian culture. The performances are distinguished by their intensity and genuineness. Guests can anticipate a spectacular evening of rhythmic footwork, exquisite guitar playing, and passionate singing. The theater also holds the Semana Flamenca de Benalmádena, a festival that showcases traditional flamenco styles with performances by well-known musicians.

Website for Booking: http://flamencocostadelsol.com/

Location: Avenida Gamonal, 6, 29630 Benalmádena

Map Direction: https://rb.gy/sogw9p

Semana Santa (Holy Week) - During Easter Week

Benalmádena comes alive with religious processions flowing through the streets of Benalmádena Pueblo and

Arroyo de la Miel. The best part is the live presentation of the Passion of Christ, also known as El Paso, held in the old village on Good Friday. Locals dressed in biblical costumes lead the parade, producing an emotionally charged show steeped in history.

Corpus Christi - Early June

Benalmádena Pueblo is transformed into a floral paradise during the Corpus Christi festivities. Residents diligently decorate the streets with over 70,000 flower stalks, forming complex carpets to pave the way for the Holy procession. This breathtaking exhibition of local artistic talent is a visual feast and a reflection of the town's passion.

San Juan Fair - June

Arroyo de la Miel's annual local fair runs from June 24th to 29th. The San Juan Fair ushers in summer with a bang. The town celebrates by staging a local fair that attracts thousands of people. Expect vibrant music, dancing, and a spectacular finale of bonfires and fireworks on the beach to commemorate the warmth of coastal nights.

Benalmádena Summer Festival - 15th - 29th July

The Summer Festival is a cultural spectacle hosted at the Parque de La Paloma Auditorium. It features a diverse range of music, theater, and dance performances. This fortnight-long event is a must-see for art lovers and the ideal way to immerse yourself in the town's creative energy under a beautiful summer sky.

Veladilla del Carmen - July 16th

The Virgen del Carmen procession is a cherished local tradition, celebrating the patron saint of sailors. The evening procession of the Virgin Carmen begins at Church Square, Avenida Bonanza. Following a special Mass, the statue of the Virgin is taken to the sea, where the procession proceeds by boat, accompanied by a flotilla. Music, dancing, and an amazing firework show over Malapesquera Beach cap up the day.

Festival of the Virgen de la Cruz - Mid-August

Great cultural significance is attached to Benalmádena's Virgen de la Cruz celebration. A customary procession through the Pueblo's streets honors the Virgin of the Cross.

It is a deep expression of faith and culture that brings the community together in worship and joy.

Please keep in mind that dates and activities are subject to change, so double-check the specifics as they approach.

Nightlife and Entertainment

Benalmádena's nightlife is as vibrant as its sunny days, with plenty of options for entertainment after dark. Here's a look at the town's vibrant night scene:

Bars, Clubs, and Live Entertainment:

Minnelli's

Minnelli's is a vibrant nightlife destination well known for its immersive and intimate drag shows. Every Sunday, the venue hosts a special Jukebox Bingo night, among other shows. Minnelli's, with its comfy booth seating and table service, creates a fantastic atmosphere in which customers can experience the art of drag in a fresh and fascinating way. Anyone looking for a night of glitter, singing, comedy, and dancing should check it out.

Website: https://minnellis.com/

Map Direction: https://rb.gy/d02pgi

Bar Ole

Bar Ole is a specialty drinks bar known for its lively ambiance and diverse cocktail menu. It is a popular venue for both tourists and locals, serving mojitos, gins, tonics, wines, beers, and spirits. The bar is well-known for its courteous service and is an excellent spot to unwind after a long day of exploration. Anyone wishing to take in the local nightlife and sample beautifully produced cocktails should check it out because of its excellent location and high reputation.

Location: Plaza Olé, 29631 Benalmádena

Map Direction: https://rb.gy/ms3q74

Opening Hours: Thursday to Sunday from 6 pm to 2 am.

L.A Bar

L.A Bar is a popular nightlife spot known for its great service and welcoming atmosphere. It is in Avenida de Antonio Machado and provides a comfortable setting with beautiful coastal views. People love to come to this pub because of how clean it is and how good the music is. Guests are made to feel at home while they sip on one of many cocktails. It's open every evening and is an excellent place to relax and socialize. If you are interested in Benalmádena's lively nightlife, you should not miss the L.A Bar.

Location: Avenida Antonio Machado, 76, 29630 Benalmádena

Map Direction: https://rb.gy/xpvkmh

Opening Hours: Monday to Friday from 7:30 pm to 1:30 am. 8 pm to 1:30 am on Saturdays.

Darcie's Motown Bar

Darcie's Motown Bar is a lively place to immerse yourself in the soulful sounds of Motown and Soul music. It is well-known for its lively atmosphere and friendly staff, making it an excellent choice for anyone searching for a night out with low-cost drinks and terrific music. It's a friendly and safe place, frequently described as one where you walk in as a stranger and go out as a friend.

Map Direction: https://rb.gy/4vlya9

Opening Hours: Wednesday to Sunday from 6 pm–2 am. Closed on Mondays.

Scanlons Shamrock Irish Pub

Scanlon's Shamrock Irish Pub is a popular nightlife spot in Benalmádena, recognized for its genuine Irish charm and welcoming environment. It is popular for its high-quality beers and spirits, which include Guinness and Heineken on tap, as well as its specialty Irish coffee. The bar is acknowledged for its pleasant staff and timely service, making it a place to have fun and laugh.

Location: Avenida Antonio Machado, 106, Edificio Benalplaya, 29630 Benalmádena

Map Direction: https://rb.gy/nlvesd

Opening Hours: 12 pm

Location: Avenida de Bonanza, 16, 29630 Benalmádena

Map Direction:

Opening Hours: Monday to Sunday 7 pm–2:45 am. Closed on Tuesdays.2 am daily.

The Mad Ass Irish Sports Bar

The Mad Ass Irish Sports Bar is a bustling hub with a lively ambiance and extensive sports coverage. It's an excellent place to watch live sporting events because of its large interior, Irish-themed decor, and outdoor patio. The bar serves a variety of meals and drinks, including cold Cruscampo lagers. It's a spot where fun and camaraderie are always on the menu.

Location: Carril del Siroco, 4, 29630 Benalmádena

Map Direction: https://rb.gy/7novhp

Opening Hours: 10 am–12 am daily.

CJ's Karaoke Bar

Cj's Karaoke Bar is a well-known karaoke spot known for its vibrant atmosphere and broad song selection, which attracts tourists as well as locals. The bar is well-known for its lively atmosphere and welcoming staff. It's the ideal spot to relax with a song after a day of exploring. Whether you are a longtime karaoke fan or a first-timer, Cj's Karaoke Bar promises a memorable night out.

Location: Avenida de Bonanza, 16, 29630 Benalmádena

Map Direction: https://rb.gy/ojketa

Opening Hours: Monday to Sunday 7 pm–2:45 am. Closed on Tuesdays.

Bonanza Bar

Bonanza Bar is a popular nightlife destination with live music and a disco vibe. It is the go-to destination for tribute acts, bands, and other performers, ensuring a wonderful night of entertainment. The bar conducts jam sessions, quiz days, bingo, and karaoke to cater to a variety of entertainment tastes. It provides over 3 hours of vivid adventures. It is well-known for its affordable drink specials and top-notch waiter service, guaranteeing a fun night for everybody. Reservations is required.

Phone: +34 611 34 38 23

Location: Avenida de Bonanza, 1, 29630 Benalmádena

Map Direction: https://rb.gy/my0t13

Opening Hours: Wednesday to Sunday from 7 pm–3 am. Closed on Mondays and Tuesdays.

Black Jack Sports and Family Bar

Black Jack Sports and Family Bar is a highly rated spot perfect for family fun and sports enthusiasts. It has a games room for all ages, a family room, and a refreshing terrace. It is wheelchair accessible, pet friendly, and has a well-stocked bar. It is about 5 minutes from Sunset Beach Hotel and is well-known for its friendly staff. The opening hours vary, with weekends providing more opportunities to enjoy the atmosphere. It's a nice place for a relaxing evening or to watch a game.

Location: Pje. del Águila, 5, 29630 Benalmádena

Map Direction: https://rb.gy/w5izp5

Opening Hours: Wednesday to Friday from 6 pm–12 am. 1 pm–10 pm on Saturday and sundays.

Tourist Traps to Avoid

It is important to exercise caution and avoid common problems that might negatively impact your Benalmádena journey. Here's a local's tip for avoiding tourist traps:

1. Beware of Overpriced Restaurants

Many eateries compete for your attention in the tourist hotspot of Benalmádena Costa. However, not all enticing menus provide culinary delights.

National flags and translations on the menu are the most obvious indication that you are about to eat at a tourist trap. These restaurants frequently favor quantity above quality, leaving your taste buds unsatisfied and your wallet lighter. Instead, look for hidden jewels in the area; ask residents for suggestions, visit the places listed in this book, or take a stroll through Benalmádena Pueblo's more tranquil streets to enjoy true Andalusian cuisine.

2. The Double-Edged Sword of Puerto Marina

Puerto Marina is a must-see because of its glittering yachts and attractive waterfront area. However, it is also a popular location for tourist traps. Keep an eye out for overpriced and substandard items as you go around the marina. Some eateries here sacrifice authenticity for convenience by serving mostly tourists. To prevent disappointment, go beyond the marina's immediate surroundings. Look for tucked-away bistros and tapas cafes in the surrounding streets where the locals eat.

3. Street Market Vigilance

Street markets are lively hubs of activity, but they can also attract pickpockets. Make sure to protect your possessions whether you are shopping for fresh vegetables or souvenirs. Keep your luggage closed and close to your body. While most market sellers are trustworthy, it is wise to exercise caution, particularly in congested places.

4. Nightclub Caution

Benalmádena's nightlife is filled with throbbing beats and bright lights. However, some nightclubs take advantage of unsuspecting tourists.

Avoid promoters who aggressively sell entry tickets or drink packages. These clubs frequently give too little for too much. Instead, get advice from fellow tourists, and locals or stick to the places listed in this book. Go for places where the music is infectious, the crowd diverse, and the vibe genuine. Also, keep an eye out for narcotics at nightclubs.

5. Check the Taxi Meter

Although taxis are an easy way to move about, some dishonest drivers could take advantage of tourists. Before beginning the journey, always make sure the meter is functioning and request an estimated fee. If you suspect an overcharge, respectfully bargain or get another cab. There are trustworthy taxi services out there, so don't allow a negative experience to ruin your impression.

6. Choose Souvenir Shops Wisely

Souvenir stores near major tourist destinations sometimes overprice their products. Refrain from making rash purchases; instead, go for a walk, evaluate prices, and consider purchasing from smaller, family-owned businesses.

Instead of mass-produced souvenirs, look for unique products that reflect Benalmádena's culture.

7. Timeshare Touts

Beware of zealous salespeople who offer free goods in return for attending a timeshare presentation. These interactions can be stressful and time-consuming. Politely refuse and concentrate on enjoying your holiday without the sales pitch.

Benalmádena's ultimate magic exists beyond the obvious. Seek authenticity, interact with people, and relish the unscripted moments for tourists. With a keen eye, you will discover the essence of this coastal gem.

CHAPTER 5

Experiencing Benalmádena's Delights

The coastal town of Benalmádena is a foodie's paradise. This place offers a wide variety of delectable and diverse cuisine, ranging from the freshest seafoods to classic Andalusian specialties. Here's how to enjoy the finest of Benalmádena's food scene.

What to eat

Benalmádena's food reflects its Mediterranean surroundings. Popular seafood recipes include pescaíto frito (fried fish) and espetos (skewered sardines cooked over a pit of coal). Try the gazpacho or salmorejo, two refreshing tomato-based soups that are ideal for warm weather, to get a taste of the region.

Enjoy the blend of traditional and modern, the fresh food, and the stunning surroundings that make eating in Benalmádena a memorable experience. Benalmádena's restaurants cater to all tastes, whether you are searching for a fine dining experience or a taste of local delicacies.

Popular Andalusian Dishes You Should Try:

Tostadas with tomato sauce and olive oil (Spanish breakfast)

Churros with chocolate

Bocadillo with local jamon (sandwich)

Patatas bravas (fried potatoes)

Gambas Pil Pil (Fried Prawns)

Gazpacho (Cold Soup)

Espetos (grilled sardines)

Rabo de Toro (bull tail stew or Oxtail Stew)

Salmorejo (cold soup)

Local Dining Options

Restaurante Da Checco & Paola

Restaurante Da Checco & Paola provides a unique dining experience with its combination of Italian and Mediterranean cuisines. The restaurant is known for its steakhouse and barbecue dishes and has a comfortable ambiance. The menu offers a variety of options for vegetarians, vegans, and those with gluten sensitivities, including tenderloin steak, pasta, pizza, and fresh seafood. To ensure a wonderful lunch, it is advisable to make a reservation at this culinary gem, which is known for its dedication to service and quality.

Location: Avenida las Palmeras, 28, 29630 Benalmádena

Map Direction: https://rb.gy/62o848

Open Hours: Tuesday to Sunday from 4 pm–11 pm

Phone: +34 608 40 87 85

The Steakhouse

The Steakhouse is a popular destination for steak lovers, with a variety of exquisite cuts grilled to perfection. The Steakhouse caters to a wide range of dietary needs with its flexible menu, which features gluten-free and regional dishes. The ambiance is sophisticated yet welcoming, making it ideal for families, couples, and groups. They have a reputation for providing dependably good meals, attentive service, and high-quality meat.

Location: Avenida Darsena de Levante local B9 Benalmadena, 29630

Map Direction: https://rb.gy/hk9zon

Open Hours: 1 pm–12 am daily.

Website: https://www.bestrestaurantsbenalmadena.com/steakhouse/

Phone: +34 952 44 20 12

Karma Mediterranean Restaurant

Karma Mediterranean Restaurant is known for its Mediterranean and European cuisine, which includes a wide range of seafood and Spanish dishes, as well as a vegetarian, vegan, and gluten-free menu. Their signature dish is Karma Halibut, and they also have a three-course meal deal that is quite reasonably priced. They are known for both quality and value, so make a reservation in advance to enjoy the restaurant's warm and inviting ambiance.

Location: Avenida las Palmeras, 6, local 13, 29630 Benalmádena

Map Direction: https://rb.gy/02qs9p

Open Hours: Monday to Sunday from 5pm–11 pm. Closed on Wednesdays.

Phone: +34 951 46 82 98

Restaurante Las Brisas

Restaurante Las Brisas is a quaint eatery that serves a delectable blend of native Spanish and Mediterranean cuisine, with a focus on fresh seafood. The restaurant is known for its superb paella, and the menu features vegetarian, vegan, and gluten-free options. It is a great option for those seeking a genuine seaside eating experience, thanks to its ideal location on Paseo Maritimo and its reputation for welcoming service.

Location: Paseo Maritimo Playa Santa Ana, 29630, Benalmadena

Map Direction: https://rb.gy/ktgmug

Opening Hours: Monday to Sunday from 12 pm–6 pm, 6:30 pm–11 pm. Closed on Wednesdays.

For Reservations: https://rb.gy/sox8uo

Phone: +34 640 09 35 74

Lime & Lemon

The lively Lime & Lemon serves a fusion of modern, Mediterranean, European, and international cuisines. They are known for their healthy menu selections, which include vegetarian, vegan, and gluten-free foods. The restaurant has a welcoming ambiance, and customers compliment the outstanding food and attentive service. It is a great choice for those looking for a diverse menu in a comfortable environment. It is recommended that you book ahead of time.

Location: edificio MAITE 1, Avenida las Palmeras, 1, 29630 Benalmádena

Map Direction: https://rb.gy/1m8g5a

Opening Hours: Wednesday to Sunday from 6 pm–10:30 pm

Website: https://www.limeandlemontapas.net/

The Drunken Sailor

The Drunken Sailor is a popular bar and restaurant that serves British and European bar food, as well as vegetarian and vegan options. The restaurant is known for its homemade food, excellent cocktails, picturesque views, and fair prices. It's a casual place where families and friends can enjoy a relaxed meal with a cozy atmosphere.

Location: 23 Las Gaviotas, Avenida Antonio Machado, 57, 29630 Benalmádena

Map Direction: https://rb.gy/wdwcoa

Opening Hours: Tuesday to Sunday from 10 am–6 pm

Phone: +34 691 85 87 48

Lillie Langtry

Lillie Langtry is a welcoming British pub with a selection of British pub food and a nice ambiance. They are known for their homemade food, including favorites like steak with peppercorn sauce and hearty burgers. The pub also serves vegetarian, vegan, and gluten-free options, so there is something for everyone. They offer suntrap outdoor seating and lively entertainment, and the owners are friendly. It is a place where good food and good times come together.

Location: Avenida Antonio Machado, 54, 29631 Benalmádena

Map Direction: https://rb.gy/ve9unf

Opening Hours: 7 pm–1 am daily.

Phone: +34 951 39 89 77

Potter's Lodge

Potter's Lodge is a nice bar and cafe that serves a variety of local dishes, British pub classics, and vegetarian options. The ambiance is cozy with good homemade meals and pleasant staff. It is a spot where you can have a relaxed meal while making use of the full bar and outdoor seating to enjoy the Spanish sunshine. The prices are reasonable for the quality provided, and they are recommended for their excellent service and value.

Location: Avenida de los Abedules, 6, 29630 Benalmádena

Map Direction: https://rb.gy/ef7c2r

Opening Hours: Monday to Friday from 12 pm–12 am

Phone: +34 675 23 41 95

Restaurante OK - Cocina Internacional

Restaurante OK - Cocina Internacional serves a broad menu that includes Mediterranean, European, Spanish, and international cuisines. They are popular for their grilled specialties and vegetarian options. For years, the eatery has been a local favorite, known for its comfort food. It is suggested to make reservations to enjoy the excellent service and traditional surroundings. It is a great choice for an international dining experience with a local touch.

Location: Calle San Francisco, 4, 29630 Benalmádena

Map Direction: https://rb.gy/a5cwhn

Opening Hours: Monday, Friday & Saturday 1:30 pm–4 pm, 7:30 pm–11 pm. Tuesday & Sunday 1:30 pm–11 pm. Closed on Wednesdays.

Phone: +34 951 45 90 36

Restaurante El Cordero

Restaurante El Cordero is a wonderful restaurant with a Mediterranean, European, and Spanish menu and is known for its affordable prices and courteous service. The restaurant offers a menu del día (menu of the day) which includes a choice of dishes, wine, and a complimentary liqueur, all at an affordable price. They offer a good menu selection and the food quality is great, making it a popular option for both locals and tourists looking for a traditional dining experience. It is recommended that you call to book in advance to avoid being disappointed.

Location: Plaza Nueva, Av. de Bonanza, 8, 29631 Arroyo de La Miel, Benalmádena

Map Direction: https://rb.gy/z1m6pz

Opening Hours: Monday to Saturday from 6 pm–12 am.

Phone: +34 952 44 77 89

Fine Dining Options

Restaurante La Perla

Restaurante La Perla is a fine dining restaurant that offers a sumptuous experience with its Mediterranean, European, and Spanish dishes. The restaurant is known for meals such as bonbon foie gras and seafood prepared with a unique touch. The restaurant caters to special events and provides vegetarian, vegan, and gluten-free options. The magnificent classic decor and stunning vistas make it a memorable dining spot.

Location: C. Ibiza, 12, 29639 Benalmádena

Map Direction: https://rb.gy/fp6wzh

Opening Hours: 7:30 pm–11:30 pm on Tuesdays. Wednesday to Saturday from 1:30 pm–4 pm, 7:30 pm–11 pm. 1:30 pm–4 pm, 7:30–10:30 pm on Sundays.

Website: https://www.restaurantelaperla.es/en-gb

The Japo Restaurant

The Japo Restaurant is a top tier eating destination, that specializes in Japanese cuisine, offering an exceptional assortment of sushi and Asian foods. The restaurant is known for its tranquil atmosphere, melt-in-your-mouth fish, and excellent service. It is a high-end option that offers a spectacular culinary experience. The taster menu coupled with wine is recommended especially for a relaxing afternoon lunch to get away from the heat.

Location: Avenida del Sol, 225b, 29631 Benalmádena

Map Direction: https://rb.gy/5a2qr7

Opening Hours: Wednesday to Sunday from 1:30 pm–4:30 pm, 7 pm–11 pm.

Website: https://www.thebeachclubhigueron.com/en/reservations/the-japo/

Escorpio Restaurante

Escorpio Restaurante is a Mediterranean paradise where sea and mountain flavors blend. It is in the La Fonda Hotel and offers a menu that is mindful of the environment with natural, seasonal ingredients. The restaurant is known for its Mediterranean cuisine, beautiful coastal views, and high-quality food and service. Its hours change daily, however it is open for lunch and dinner. The menu includes meals like Ensaladilla Rusa and Fideos tostados.

Location: C. Maestro García Álvarez, 29639 Benalmádena

Map Direction: https://rb.gy/joupgm

Opening Hours: Monday, Wednesday & Sunday 1:30 pm–4 pm. Thursday to Saturday 1:30–4 pm, 7:30–10:30 pm. Closed on Tuesdays.

For Reservations: https://rb.gy/35vk7k

Restaurante Carmesí Benalmádena pueblo

Restaurante Carmesí, a fine-dining French restaurant, has quickly become a local favorite. The restaurant is known for its excellent menu, impeccable service, and pleasant atmosphere. The chef's amazing inventions and second-to-none service set it apart. The restaurant is recommended to experience fresh, well-thought-out dishes and to enjoy the calm atmosphere with a touch of Dutch coolness. It is the perfect place for an evening dinner to remember.

Location: Avenida del Chorrillo, 29639 Benalmádena

Map Direction: https://rb.gy/99wfdo

Opening Hours: Tuesday to Sunday from 7 pm-11:30 pm

Website: https://restaurantecarmesi.eatbu.com/?lang=en

Budget Dining

Taperia La Bodeguita

Taperia La Bodeguita is a modest restaurant that serves Mediterranean, Spanish, and European cuisine. It is known for its cozy environment and tasty homemade tapas. With reasonably priced tapas, it is a good deal for those who want to try many meals. The restaurant is small, but the experience is big. Snails and tripe & chorizo tapas are recommended for a genuine flavor. It is an excellent choice for a casual and friendly dining experience.

Location: Avenida Antonio Machado, 80, 29630 Benalmádena

Map Direction: https://rb.gy/b63tom

Opening Hours: Monday to Friday from 9:30 am–11:30 pm. Saturdays from 9:30 am–6 pm.

Phone: +34 952 57 74 41

Stentons

Stentons is a British café and pub that is known for its Build Your Own Breakfast, homemade cheesecakes, and Sunday roasts. It serves freshly prepared British cuisine in a pleasant ambiance. The menu offers gluten-free and vegetarian alternatives to ensure a friendly environment for all. They offer excellent value for money and serve quality traditional British fare. It is a great spot for a satisfying meal, with a full bar and outdoor seating available.

Location: Calle Sagitario, Block 9, Local 8/9, 29631 Benalmádena

Map Direction: https://rb.gy/a3fb6t

Opening Hours: Monday to Sunday from 10 am–7 pm. Closed on Wednesdays.

Phone: +34 952 19 11 15

Restaurante Los Delantales

Restaurante Los Delantales is a fantastic option if you are looking for authentic Moroccan and Mediterranean flavors. It is the place to go for pastela, couscous, and kefta meatballs. The restaurant is known for its halal dishes and vegetarian-friendly options, which make every guest feel welcome. This restaurant is recommended for its relaxed atmosphere and excellent value for money.

Location: Calle San Telmo, 20, 29631 Arroyo de La Miel, Benalmádena

Map Direction: https://rb.gy/adqi1c

Opening Hours: Monday to Sunday from 12 pm–4:30 pm, 7:30 pm–12 am.

Website: https://www.restaurantelosdelantales.com/

Lo Spritz One Arroyo de la Miel

Lo Spritz One Arroyo de la Miel is a cozy pizzeria known for its authentic Italian dishes and friendly staff. The restaurant serves a range of pizzas with customizable toppings, as well as other Italian staples such as cannelloni with spinach. It is recommended for its excellent meals and service. It's a beautiful place for a casual meal, offering both dine-in and takeout choices.

Location: Bloque 2, Residencial Madrid, Avenida Federico García Lorca, 37, Local 4, 29631 Arroyo de La Miel.

Map Direction: https://rb.gy/1gp9j0

Opening Hours: Wednesday - Sunday: 1:30pm - 4:00pm & 7 pm - 11 pm.

Website: https://lospritzonepizzeria.com/

Restaurant No.7

Restaurant No.7 is a British pub and café that specializes in British cuisine. They serve a range of meals, including a chef's special handcrafted steak and Guinness pie. The restaurant offers vegetarian, vegan, and gluten-free dishes to accommodate various dietary preferences. It's a comfortable place for breakfast, lunch, supper, or cocktails, with pleasant English-speaking staff and moderate costs. They are known for their generous portions, and making a reservation is recommended for an enjoyable dining experience.

Location: Avenida Antonio Machado, 29631 Benalmádena.

Map Direction: https://rb.gy/62xdr8

Opening Hours: Monday to Saturday from 9 am–3 pm, 6 pm–10 pm. Sundays from 9 am–9 pm

Phone: +34 655 03 68 27

Cuisine Adventures

Indulge in a gastronomic experience in Benalmádena, where the aromas of the Mediterranean meet the fiery flavors of international cuisine. This seaside jewel provides a gourmet adventure that tantalizes the senses while also satisfying the spirit. You can also attend a cooking lesson to learn more about the region's cuisine and culture.

Spanish Cooking Lessons: This is for you if you want to taste authentic Spanish and local cuisine, as well as learn how to cook Spanish dishes like Paella and prawn Pil-Pil. Take a private cooking session in a charming avant-garde kitchen in the heart of Benalmadena's Puerto Marina. The local chef will teach you how to cook like a Spaniard.

Location: C. La Fragata, Local B6, Planta Baja, 29630 Benalmádena

Direction: https://rb.gy/sjmi8t

Phone: +34 659 026 656

Website for booking: https://www.spanishcookinglessons.com/

Argentinian Flavors - Asador El Quebracho: Enjoy traditional asado techniques with dishes like Entraña and Vacio that take you to the vibrant streets of Buenos Aires. They provide delicious meals in a wonderful restaurant. The steaks are fantastic, the wine list is terrific, and the service is outstanding.

Location: Avenida las Palmeras, 6, 29630 Benalmádena

Map Direction: https://rb.gy/8k5u2q

Opening Hours: 12:30 pm–10:30 pm on Monday, Wednesday, Thursday & Sunday. 12:30 pm–11 pm on Friday & Saturday

Website: https://www.asadorelquebracho.es/

Taste of Northern Spain - Rincón Asturiano: Indulge yourself in Asturian culture with satisfying dishes like the Fabe Asturiana, a bean stew that captures the essence of the region. This restaurant is highly recommended for its excellent food, hospitality, and setting.

Location: Avenida de la Estación s/n Ctro. Ccial Plaza Iglesia, Local 4, 29631 Benalmádena.

Map Direction: https://rb.gy/al53h1

Opening Hours: Wednesday to Saturday from 1 pm–4 pm, 7:30–11 pm.

1 pm–4 pm on Sunday.

Phone: +34 952 56 76 28

Wine & Dine - La Despensa Tapas and Wine Bar: Enjoy a night of exquisite wines matched with gastronomic delights such as local Spanish tapas, handmade cheeses, and the best cuts of jamón. The restaurant has excellent wine, terrific food, welcoming service, and a wonderful atmosphere reminiscent of traditional Spanish family dinners.

Location: Avenida las Palmeras, 21, 29631 Arroyo de La Miel,

Map Direction: https://rb.gy/37h4i7

Opening Hours: 11 am–1 am daily.

Phone: +34 952 56 01 99

Shopping in Benalmádena

Shopping in Benalmádena is an enjoyable experience that combines classic Spanish charm with modern convenience. Here's what to anticipate whether you are shopping for local produce clothing, or souvenirs:

Puerto Marina Shopping

Here is the commercial district of Benalmádena which boasts an assortment of boutiques, restaurants, and shops with a view of the marina.

Location: Puerto Deportivo de Benalmadena, Av. del Puerto Deportivo, s/n, 29630 Benalmádena.

Map Direction: https://rb.gy/ylae34

Opening Hours: 10:30 am–12 am daily.

Website: https://puertomarinashopping.es/

Arroyo De La Miel

Arroyo De La Miel is one of the three villages comprising the Benalmadena. It is a lively neighborhood with local stores providing anything from apparel to handcrafted items.

Map Direction: https://rb.gy/0dkc6i

Bonanza Square

It is a bustling plaza full of pubs, taverns, and restaurants, both day and night. Here provides a calmer shopping experience with a variety of modest businesses and eateries.

Map Direction: https://rb.gy/5v35hw

The Promenade

The Promenade begins from Castillo Bil Bil and spans 2.3 kilometers to the marina. Ideal for a stroll, the area is packed with stores selling beachwear, accessories, and souvenirs.

If you are looking for a more traditional shopping experience, try your hand at haggling at one of the local markets, such as the one in Paloma Park. Be sure to factor in siesta time while planning your shopping excursion, as many stores, especially smaller ones, close in the afternoon.

Two large outdoor markets in Benalmadena provide locals and tourists with various shopping options. The first of these markets is held on Wednesdays from 9 a.m. to 2 p.m. at the upper area of the Paloma Park car park. The second market is held on Fridays from 9 a.m. to 2 p.m. in the Tivoli car park in the Arroyo de la Miel area.

There is a wide variety of goods available at these markets, so it's a great place to find something that suits your taste. One way to describe the Wednesday market is as a bustling flea market, selling a wide variety of interesting and, frequently, antique goods. The Friday market, on the other hand, is a more typical Costa del Sol market that sells a variety of things such as fresh produce, apparel, and accessories.

Bargaining Tips and Shopping Etiquette

Shopping in Benalmádena is a fun experience, and understanding a few negotiating tricks and shopping etiquette will help make it even better. Here's a guide to assist you explore the local markets and stores:

Bargaining Tips:

Start Friendly: Start the negotiation with a warm greeting and a smile.

Know the Value: To determine when you are receiving a good deal, check the average pricing of the products beforehand.

Start Low: Make an offer that is somewhat less than what you are willing to pay, but not so much that the seller will take offense.

Be Polite: Even if you are not interested in the seller's final offer, you should always be polite.

Walk Away: If the price is not reasonable, do not be scared to walk away. This may occasionally prompt the vendor to offer a lower price.

Cash is King: Cash payments can sometimes aid in negotiating a better price, as it eliminates card charges for the vendor.

Shopping Etiquette

Be mindful of Siesta Time: Schedule your shopping appropriately since many stores close in the afternoon for siesta.

Greet the shopkeeper: Greeting the store owner when you walk in is considered nice.

Ask before photographing: Get permission before taking any pictures of the products or store.

Handle With Care: Be careful handling the product; you might have to purchase it if you break it.

Learn a Few Spanish Phrases: Being able to communicate in basic Spanish will improve your shopping experience and demonstrate your appreciation for the local way of life.

The key to successful negotiation is finding a balance between getting a fair deal and respecting the vendor's business.

CHAPTER 6

Day Trips from Benalmádena

Málaga

It would be a pity to visit Costa del Sol without visiting its biggest city, Malaga. You can see a lot of sites in a brief day trip, and they are all within walking distance.

For those who are interested in art, there is a museum dedicated to Picasso's birthplace, and you can also view some of his artwork at the Picasso Museum.

Outdoor enthusiasts should definitely see the Alcazaba, a stunning Moorish palace that will transport you through time with its rich history and intricate architecture. Don't miss the close-by Castillo Gibralfaro, either. The Malaga Cathedral and Muelle Uno (the port) are two more sights you should include on your itinerary.

If you want traditional Malaga cuisine, go to Mercado de Atarazanas. The market sells the finest local products and cozy bars where you can enjoy a variety of delicacies, such as fried fish (pescaito frito) and Spanish-style Russian salad (ensaladilla rusa), with a drink of wine or beer.

The Renfe Cercanías train is the fastest means to reach Malaga, taking only 30 minutes, whereas driving may take longer due to traffic. It is, nevertheless, easy to drive from Benalmadena to Malaga.

Fuengirola

From Benalmadena, Fuengirola is a simple day trip destination with lots of activities.

If you are coming with or without children, it is worth taking the short train ride to Bioparc Fuengirola. It is not your typical zoo; the park was built in the heart of the city to provide a safe sanctuary for animals while also contributing to the education and conservation of endangered species. Rather than a zoo housing animals, it gives the impression of walking into a tropical jungle or botanical garden. Adult tickets cost 24.50 euros, while children's tickets cost 18 euros and are free for kids under the age of three. Other options for families with children include Sould Park Fuengirola, a modest theme park near the harbor, and Aquamijas Water Park during the summer months.

Castillo Sohail is a must-see site in Fuengirola. This castle is on a hill and provides stunning views of the the coastline. Entry is free, and it's a popular location for festivals and performances.

It takes less than 20 minutes to drive from Benalmadena to Fuengirola, alternatively, you can use the local, quick, and affordable C-1 train.

Mijas Pueblo

Mijas Pueblo is a fantastic day trip destination near Benalmadena. Not only is it close, but there are numerous exciting things to do there.

You don't need a whole day to tour Mijas, a half-day would be enough. Enjoy a lunch outside while strolling through the charming white-painted, cobblestone walkways adorned with lovely flowerpots. You can also browse the little stores for handcrafted ceramic pots and dishes.

Not only that, but you can visit the chocolate museum and take in the breathtaking views from the overlook near the shrine. If you are a nature enthusiast, you ought to check out the lovely hiking trails in the neighborhood too.

Benalmadena to Mijas Pueblo is approximately a 25-minute journey. The shortest way to get there is to take AP-7 and A-368. Just be warned that the road is steep. If you are taking public transportation, board the M-112 bus from Puerto Marina.

Marbella

In the Costa del Sol, this seaside town is a popular tourist attraction. Marbella is well-known for its lavish resorts and busy nightlife, but it also has attractive old town streets and stunning beaches.

In Marbella, Puerto Banús is among the most lavish areas. Shop for designer clothing and jewelry, have a meal al fresco, and view Ferraris and pricey boats here. During the peak season, you could prefer to relax at Cabopino Beach or visit an elite beach club like Nikki Beach Marbella.

But if you want to see Marbella in a more genuine way, you should go to the old town. Marbella's old town is a charming maze of whitewashed streets lined with unique stores, historical landmarks, and charming flowerpots hung from the walls. There is something to do in every area of the town.

The travel from Benalmadena to Marbella takes around 40 minutes. Taking the AP-7, a toll road by car, is the quickest route to Marbella. The bus from Puerto Marina is another option, although it takes longer.

Nerja

Nerja is a coastal town with beautiful beaches and the popular Nerja Caves, which display prehistoric murals and natural forms. Some of Malaga's top beaches, including Playa de Maro and Playa Burriana, are located in the town. Playa de Maro is ideal for water activities like kayaking and snorkeling.

Nerja offers much more than just beaches; you can explore the ancient center, take in views of Balcón de Europa, and explore the Museo de Nerja and Nerja Caves. If you like to explore rather than rest on the beach, Frigiliana should be on your list. The small village is only a 10-minute drive from Nerja, and it has been acknowledged as one of the most beautiful towns in Spain. Visit Frigiliana's old town and stroll through its quaint, whitewashed streets and enjoy tapas on a rooftop patio.

It takes around an hour to drive from Benalmadena to Nerja. If you are driving, use the A-7 route, which takes around an hour. If you use public transportation, take the Renfe train to Malaga and then the bus to Nerja from the Malaga bus terminal. This latter approach is significantly more time-consuming. Alternatively, you can take this Nerja Caves Tour with Frigiliana from Benalmadena. Book online here: https://rb.gy/8rdhvr

Caminito del Rey

Caminito del Rey is a breathtaking natural wonder and the most picturesque hiking path in the Malaga Province. This exciting stroll down a gorge gives adventurers breathtaking vistas and an adrenaline rush. This trail down the El Chorro gorge is a breathtaking experience not to be missed.

This hiking walk has breathtaking views of rocks, a valley, a river, and a hanging bridge. The only drawback of Caminito del Rey is that you have to get your tickets months in advance or you won't be able to go.

The A-357 road takes around 1 hour and 10 minutes to get from Benalmadena to Caminito del Rey. Should you choose not to drive and are staying in Benalmadena, a local tour company will come to you from the city center, transport you to the charming town of Ardales for breakfast, and then accompany you on a hike down the well-known Caminito del Rey with a local guide. Book online here: https://rb.gy/sxem9e

Ronda

You can tour Ronda's key attractions in a single day, and it is a stunning white town situated on a hillside. Ronda's Bridge is the first thing that springs to mind when people think of Ronda, and Puente Nuevo, one of the oldest bullrings in Spain, is the main attraction in the town.

But there are a ton of other things to do in Ronda, including hiking, visiting the archeological museum, and feasting on local foods. In addition to being well-known for its wines, Ronda is among the top destinations to discover more about the region's wine industry and sample some of Malaga's classic wines, such as Malaga sweet wine (vino dulce de Málaga).

While Ronda is certainly worth a full day's visit, you may also wish to visit Setenil de las Bodegas that same day. It is a unique village around 20 minutes drive from Ronda. Some of the dwellings are constructed within caves.

Car travel is the most convenient mode of transportation between Benalmadena and Ronda. Route A-357 and A-367, which take around one hour and twenty minutes to travel, are the most efficient and quickest.

Gibraltar

Gibraltar provides a unique blend of cultures, duty-free shopping, and the popular Rock of Gibraltar. Go to Gibraltar if you fancy checking off another country on your travel bucket list. Gibraltar is a small nation, so you can explore the main sites in less than a day.

Visit the Rock of Gibraltar and the Upper Nature Reserve, which has St Michael's Cave and other fascinating historical sites, as well as cheeky macaques and stunning vistas of Africa and Spain. You could also wish to head to Catalan Bay, a nice smaller beach, or have a boat ride.

Gibraltar also happens to be a popular day-trip destination for shoppers. Items are less expensive than in Spain and other nations since taxes are not included.

Driving from Benalmadena to Gibraltar takes around one hour and thirty minutes, making it the fastest route. Follow the AP-7, a toll road. Although it takes three hours, you can also take the Avanza L-313 bus at Puerto Marina. Outside driving, booking a tour is the next best alternative. Book online here: https://rb.gy/xlnmp4

Granada

Granada is one of Andalusia's most attractive cities. Even if a single day in Granada is not long enough to explore everything this city has to offer, you can tour its most important historical structures and enjoy its lively ambiance.

One of the few attractions you should not miss on a day trip to Granada is Alhambra, Spain's most popular Moorish palace complex. Visiting the Alhambra is a one-of-a-kind experience that could easily take up half a day. The Cathedral of Granada is another ancient structure you might wish to check off your list. If you have time, you should also explore Albaicin's lovely streets, have some mouthwatering tapas, and visit Mirador de San Nicolás to see the sunset. Visit Ysla Bakery if you are craving something sweet, they serve a variety of delicious cakes and pastries, which includes the classic piononos.

It takes approximately one hour and thirty-five minutes to drive from Benalmadena to Granada via the A-92, a toll road. This is the most straightforward route. There is also the option of taking the train from Benalmadena to Malaga, where you can get a bus to Granada from the coach station. Or you can book a guided tour at https://rb.gy/3o8cn3

Tarifa

The very first thing that springs to mind about Tarifa is the long stretches of golden sandy beaches. It is among Europe's top surfing destinations because of its amazing beaches with dunes and favorable weather. Tarifa is an ideal destination for water sports enthusiasts, and you can even go on a horseback ride on the beach.

Aside from the beaches, the town has more to offer and is worth a visit. You can visit significant structures like the Castle of Tarifa, stroll along its lovely streets, and savor a few tapas while people-watching on an outdoor patio. If you enjoy archeology, visiting Baelo Claudia is highly recommended. It is a 20-minute journey from Tarifa, but it's worth it. You will discover more about the ancient culture and view one of the best-preserved Roman cities in the region.

The fastest route to Tarifa from Benalmadena is by car, taking around one hour and forty-five minutes via AP-7. While public transportation is an option, it requires changing buses, making it less of a day trip.

Torremolinos

If you do not want to get behind the wheel or take a trip, you could just take a walk to Torremolinos.

The day excursion might only need a ten-minute stroll, for instance, from the marina, this depends on where you are lodging. You will like Torremolinos' serene atmosphere, expansive beaches, and lovely coastline. Up on the hillside, there is an ancient village with taverns and pubs around each turn.

Benalmadena is close to some of the best places to visit on the Costa del Sol. The best method to get to these destinations is by automobile because it allows you to move whenever you wish. Some of these locations are impossible to reach by public transportation or just take too long.

If you use public transportation, plan a day excursion to Torremolinos, Mijas Pueblo, Fuengirola, Marbella, or Malaga. For the most up-to-date information on public transport, visit official transportation websites or local stations.

Kindly note that I am not affiliated to the guided tour providers, they are only included to provide you with more options to enhance your day trip experience.

CHAPTER 7

Ensuring a Safe and Enjoyable Stay

A wonderful vacation experience depends on having a safe and happy stay in Benalmádena. Ensuring a safe and happy stay in Benalmádena entails being health conscious, practicing good hygiene, and knowing how to seek assistance in the event of an emergency. To help you move around the town with grace and confidence, this book offers vital advice as well as insights into local norms and customs. Following these rules will ensure a safe and happy stay in Benalmádena, letting you to completely immerse yourself in the local culture and lifestyle.

Staying Safe and Legal

Benalmádena is typically a safe site for tourists. However, like with any major tourist destination, it is prudent to remain attentive, particularly in congested places, to avoid pickpocketing. Keep a watch on your valuables whether at the beach, shopping, or taking public transportation. While drug-related crimes have increased in the region, they are limited to certain places, and tourists are unlikely to experience such problems. Driving in Benalmádena may be enjoyable, but stay aware of local traffic rules and speed restrictions to avoid penalties and maintain safety.

Cultural Etiquettes & Customs

Understanding and respecting local customs will enhance your experience in Benalmádena. Greetings are usually warm and personal, followed by a handshake or a kiss on both cheeks. Except in more formal settings, it is often okay to dress casually. It is appreciated that you are dressing for the occasion. Tipping is common at restaurants and bars, generally around 10% of the cost. Many shops may close during the siesta, so plan your shopping expeditions appropriately.

Religious practice and etiquette

Similar to much of Spain, Benalmádena has a strong Catholic background, and religious celebrations and holidays are engrained in the local way of life. The most important religious event is the Holy Week procession, which is held with great devotion. Visitors are welcome to observe these processions, but they must do so respectfully, in quiet, and without flash photography. Dress modestly and show respect when you visit places of worship, such as the local churches or the Benalmádena Stupa.

Health Tips and Insurance

Keeping yourself safe is of utmost importance when you go out on your Benalmádena journey. Here are important health tips for a worry-free stay:

Stay hydrated: The sun in the Mediterranean can be obstinate. To keep hydrated, carry a refillable water bottle and sip it regularly. Local stores sell freshly squeezed orange juice, which is a delicious way to relieve your thirst.

Sunscreen routine: Sunscreen is not just a recommendation; it is your skin's knight in shining armor. Even on overcast days, liberally apply before leaving the house. You will be grateful to yourself in the future. Because of the strong Spanish sun, protect yourself from heatstroke by wearing a hat, using sunscreen with a high SPF, and drinking enough of water.

Siesta Time: Embrace the Spanish siesta custom. The town pauses gently from 2 PM to 5 PM. Do the same—take a sleep, sip sangria, or stroll through shaded streets. This noon rest will be beneficial to both your body and spirit.

Moderate tapas consumption: While tapas are delicious, they should only be consumed in moderation. Enjoy these little meals filled with flavor, but don't overeat. Combine them with local wine or a pleasant tinto de verano.

Tap water: The tap water in Benalmádena is typically safe to drink, however if you have a sensitive stomach, go with bottled water.

Food safety: Enjoy the local cuisine, but only at reputed restaurants to avoid foodborne disease.

Insurance

Accidents occur, even in paradise. Prepare with adequate travel insurance. Here's why these matters:

1. Medical Emergency: If you require medical assistance, insurance will cover hospital visits, doctor consultations, and drugs. Believe us when we say that you would rather tour the Alcazaba fortress than worry about medical expenditures.

2. Trip cancellations: Life can be unpredictable. Insurance ensures you won't be left high and dry if unanticipated events cause you to postpone your vacation. Whether it's a family emergency or a travel inconvenience, your investment is safe.

3. Lost Luggage: Imagine your swimsuit disappearing into the baggage claim Bermuda Triangle. Insurance provides compensation for lost, delayed, or stolen luggage. You will still go to the beach in elegance.

4. Travel Delays: Flight delays occur. If you are stuck, insurance will pay your additional expenditures, such as meals and lodging. Make an unplanned mini adventure out of a delay.

Insurance is your safety net; it should not be considered an afterthought. Before flying to Benalmádena, make sure you have a trustworthy policy in place.

Hygiene: Staying Fresh and Clean

Keeping your hygiene in check will guarantee that you completely experience the enchantment of this coastal paradise throughout Benalmádena's sun-filled days and colorful nights. Let's look at some practical ways to keep fresh and tidy during your visit:

Daily routines:

Shower Power: Start the day with a revitalizing shower. The Mediterranean sun may cause you to sweat but don't worry—lather up and you will feel revitalized.

Oral Care: Brush your teeth after meals to keep your beautiful whites sparkling. Minty-fresh breath is your hidden weapon for socializing with other tourists.

Sunscreen and Skin Love:

Sunscreen Vigilance: Make sure to cover every nook and cranny of your skin with sunscreen before heading outside. As you enjoy the seaside glow, shield your skin from UV radiation.

Post-Sun Soothing: If the sun kisses you too passionately, aloe vera gel is your best friend. It soothes sun-kissed skin while whispering, you are still fabulous.

Beach Etiquette:

Sand-Free Feet: Use the available showers to wash your feet after your adventures on the sandy beach. Sand between your toes is nice; sand in your bed, not so much.

Saltwater Rinse: A swim in the Mediterranean? Yes, please. However, subsequently, rinse off the saltwater. Your skin will appreciate you.

Beach Safety: Use the designated trash cans to keep beaches tidy, and shower off after swimming to get rid of salt and sand.

Wardrobe:

Light and Breezy: Choose lightweight, breathable materials. In the fight against humidity, linen, and cotton are your friends.

Change into fresh clothes after a day of exploring. Your clothes, too, deserve to look great on vacation.

Hand hygiene:

Bring hand sanitizer for on-the-go hygiene. Clean hands are your passport to adventure, whether you are touching historic walls or eating tapas.

Footwear:

Flip-flops and Sandals: Wear comfortable footwear to match the laid-back atmosphere. Flip-flops and sandals allow your feet to breathe and move freely on cobblestone streets.

Hair Care:

Saltwater Tresses: Saltwater is a great texturizer for your hair. When it is time to leave the beach, rinse your hair to keep it shiny.

Emergency Contacts

It is a good idea to have a safety net in place even if Benalmádena promises thrills in the sun. Emergencies do not wait for convenient times. Save these important emergency contacts:

Medical Emergency:

Emergency Services (Ambulance): Call 112 for emergency medical assistance. Whether it is a sudden sickness or an accident, skilled personnel will respond quickly.

Police and law enforcement:

National Police: For non-urgent issues, dial 091. They are the people you should contact in the event of theft, missing property, or little mishaps.

Guardia Civil: For problems on highways or rural regions, dial 062. They deal with traffic accidents and other issues.

Consulate / Embassy:

Find your country's consulate or embassy. They help with passports, legal concerns, and emergencies. Keep their contact details handy.

Sustainability Tips for Responsible Travel in Benalmádena

As the sun-kissed beaches of Benalmádena beckon, let us go on an adventure that not only fills our spirits but also treads gently on this wonderful planet. Eco-tourism is a dedication to protecting the natural beauty we love, not just a trendy term. Here are some useful sustainability recommendations for your Benalmádena trip:

Respect Nature and Wildlife

Leave No Trace: Whether you are hiking in the Sierra de Mijas or walking along the shore, remember the golden rule: leave no trace. Take out what you bring in, and discard waste properly.

Birdwatching Etiquette: The birds of Benalmádena, including hoopoes, swifts, and seagulls, are beautiful creatures and should be respected. Always maintain a respectful distance, avoid disrupting nests, and never feed wildlife.

Choose Sustainable Accommodations

Eco-Friendly Hotels: Look for lodgings that value sustainability. Look for certificates such as Green Key and EarthCheck. These hotels conserve energy, reduce waste, and contribute to local communities.

Local Guesthouses: Consider staying in a beautiful guesthouse or a family-run bed and breakfast. You will not only enjoy real Andalusian hospitality, but your stay will also have a direct impact on the local economy.

Choose Eco-Friendly Transportation

Walk and Cycle: Benalmádena's small layout encourages exploring on foot or by bike. Take a stroll around the Pueblo, ride your bike down the promenade, and take in the scenery without generating any carbon emissions.

Public transportation: Take the local bus or train. They link Benalmádena to the surrounding towns and attractions. It also provides an opportunity to meet locals.

Support Local Businesses

Farmers' Markets: Experience the tastes of Andalusia at the weekly markets. Purchase fresh produce, handmade cheeses, and olive oils straight from local farmers.

Craftsmanship: Visit the craft stores in Benalmádena Pueblo. Handcrafted pottery and woven fabrics, among other treasures, are thoughtful souvenirs.

Water Wisdom

Use refillable bottles to stay hydrated in the hot Mediterranean heat. Bring a reusable water bottle and refill it at public fountains. Refrain from using single-use plastics.

Ocean Respect: While swimming or snorkeling, observe the aquatic life without disturbing it. Avoid handling corals and collecting shells.

Cultural Integration

Learn the language: A simple Hola or Gracias goes a long way. Engage with the people, learn about their customs, and enjoy the warmth of Andalusian culture.

Flamenco Nights: See a flamenco performance. The passion, rhythm, and spirit of this art form will captivate you.

Responsible dining

Seafood Options: Fresh seafood is abundant along Benalmádena's shore. Choose responsibly sourced seafood and support local fishermen.

Tapas Consciousness: Enjoy tapas thoughtfully. To help reduce food waste, order only what you can finish.

Reduce Plastic Use

BYOB (Bring Your Own Bag): When shopping, bring a reusable tote bag. Plastic bags endanger marine life and litter the ecosystem.

Say No to Straws: When drinking sangria, skip the plastic straw. Request a drink without a straw.

Take part in the cleanup efforts

Beach Clean-ups: Participate in local projects or arrange your own beach cleanup. Every bit of rubbish cleared has an impact.

Volunteer opportunities: Check whether there are any eco-volunteering opportunities during your visit. Plant trees, repair paths, or help safeguard endangered animals.

Spread the Word

Share Your Journey: Encourage others to travel sustainably. Share your eco-friendly experiences in Benalmádena. Let's start a chain reaction of mindful travelers.

It is up to us all to preserve Benalmádena's beauty. Let us explore, enjoy, and safeguard this coastal gem, one mindful step at a time.

Enjoy Your Vacation...

Travel Planner

Destination: _____

Date: _____

Budget: _____

To Do	Food Must Try
	Place To Visit
	Notes

More About Your Experience

Travel Planner

Destination: _____

Date: _____

Budget: _____

To Do

Food Must Try

Place To Visit

Notes

More About Your Experience

Travel Planner

Destination: _____

Date: _____

Budget: _____

To Do

Food Must Try

Place To Visit

Notes

More About Your Experience

Travel Planner

Destination: _____

Date: _____

Budget: _____

To Do	Food Must Try
	Place To Visit
	Notes

More About Your Experience

Travel Planner

Destination: _____

Date: _____

Budget: _____

To Do	Food Must Try
	Place To Visit
	Notes

More About Your Experience

Travel Planner

Destination: _____

Date: _____

Budget: _____

To Do	Food Must Try

	Place To Visit

	Notes

More About Your Experience

Travel Planner

Destination: _____

Date: _____

Budget: _____

To Do	Food Must Try
	Place To Visit
	Notes

More About Your Experience

Travel Planner

Destination: _____

Date: _____

Budget: _____

To Do	Food Must Try
	Place To Visit
	Notes

More About Your Experience

Travel Planner

Destination: _____

Date: _____

Budget: _____

To Do	Food Must Try
	Place To Visit
	Notes

More About Your Experience

Travel Planner

Destination: _____

Date: _____

Budget: _____

To Do	Food Must Try
	Place To Visit
	Notes

More About Your Experience

Printed in Great Britain
by Amazon